Contracts Outline
Elite law school notes

By Kevin Lomax, JD

Copyright © 2020 Kevin Lomax

All rights reserved. This book or any portion thereof may not be reproduced or used in any manner whatsoever without the express written permission of the publisher.

Disclaimer: This book does not in any way establish or recommend any legal guidelines or legal practice. The information presented in this book is solely intended to be used for exam preparation and not for representing clients. I take no responsibility for any errors you may make using the information presented in this book.

Preface

I wrote this outline when I was a student at a top ten law school. I spent over 100 hours working on it, in fact, perfecting it. I used it to ace the class, and in the process learned to study smarter, not harder. Use this outline, in addition to reading the cases assigned to you, with an emphasis on *really* knowing this outline come exam time. I am confident with this outline you too now have the tool to ace your class!

OFFER AND ACCEPTANCE: MUTUAL ASSENT

A. MUTUAL ASSENT: DEFINED AND DISCUSSED
  i. For a contract to be valid, the parties must manifest a **mutual assent to be bound** [Rest. §18]. It is necessary to show that one party wished to exchange a particular item or service for specified terms, and that the other party agreed to that exchange
B. MUTUAL ASSENT JUDGED BY OBJECTIVE TEST
  i. Whether mutual assent has been achieved is judged by the **objective theory of contracts**, i.e., whether a *reasonable* person would conclude that a contract had been formed
  ii. Elimination of C/L "Meeting of the Minds"
    1. It is only important that a reasonable person in the position of one party would conclude that the other party intended to be bound **even if at the time that party did not intend to be contractually bound**
    2. Ex: *Hawkins v. McGee*. Surgeon tells parents of a boy that he would "guarantee" to make boy's hand "100% perfect" if the parents agreed to contract for his services. At trial, doctor claimed he did not intend for his statements to act as a contractual commitment, esp. in light of all his warnings that it was experimental treatment. **Held**: The question of whether the doctor had entered into a contract with the parents is one for the jury to determine under an objective test. Jury concluded that a reasonable person in the position of the parents would believe that the doctor made an offer to be legally bound to produce a 100% perfect hand, and parents accepted offer, a contract was formed, regardless of whether the doctor subjectively believed he had made a contractual promise to cure the hand
  iii. Presumption against mutual assent to contract in domestic or social situations
C. PRECISE TIME OF MAKING OF CONTRACT IRRELEVANT FOR DETERMINING MUTUAL ASSENT
  i. So long as mutual intent to be bound can be found at *any* point in time, a valid contract is formed. **Mutuality of obligation can still be satisfied even if the precise moment of contract formation cannot be precisely determined** [Rest. §22(2); UCC §2-204(2)]
D. MUTAL ASSENT TO ALL TERMS NOT REQUIRED
  i. It is only necessary that there be agreement as to the **essential terms**

II. **OFFER AND ACCEPTANCE: OFFERS**

A. OFFER: DEFINED AND DISCUSSED

        i. An "offer" is the manifestation by one party (the offeror) of a willingness to enter into a bargain with another (the offeree) on certain terms. To be a valid offer, the manifestation must raise a reasonable expectation *in the offeree* that *nothing more than acceptance is needed* by the offeree to create a contract [Rest. §24]. Offers can be written, oral, or expressed by conduct. In a simple negotiation, offers are typically the *next-to-last communication* before contract formation (acceptances being the last), but in complicated, long-distance negotiations, it may be difficult to pinpoint exactly which document or draft was an offer

B. EFFECT OF AN OFFER
        i. A valid offer creates in the offeree the **power of acceptance**. This allows the offeree to conclude a contract merely by accepting a valid, outstanding offer

C. TEST TO DETERMINE WHETHER AN "OFFER" WAS MADE: THE OBJECTIVE THEORY OF CONTRACTS
        i. Whether an "offer" has been made is judged by **whether a reasonable person, in the position of the offeree**, would believe that only his expression of assent is necessary to form an enforceable contract
       ii. In making the determination as to whether an offer was made, it is important to consider both the specific words and conduct of the offeror, and the context in which such words or actions were made
      iii. Distinguishing offers from other types of communications
          1. Offer distinguished from Statement of Future Intention
             a. A statement that a party is thinking about making an offer, or may be willing to be bound in the future, is not an offer. [Rest. §26, Com. d]
          2. Offer distinguished from Requests for Price Quotation
             a. When someone merely asks for a **price quotation**, no offer is made, for there is no manifestation to be bound
          3. Offer distinguished from a Preliminary Negotiation or Invitation to Make an Offer
             a. A statement that solicits the other party to make an offer is not an offer itself, but rather a **preliminary negotiation** or **invitation to make an offer** [Rest. §26]
             b. Ex: Dutch tells Raman, "Would you consider selling your Benz for $36,000?" and Raman responds, "Sold". There is no contract for it is Raman, not Dutch, who has made the offer
          4. Offer distinguished from Advertisements/Catalogue Descriptions
             a. An advertisement or a description in a catalogue is not an offer, but rather a solicitation to make an

offer. Thus, it is the reader who is deemed to make an offer when he tries to purchase an item
- b. Exception: If the advertisement or catalogue description (1) specifies a particular quantity of goods to be offered at the invited price AND (2) indicates to an offeree what specific steps need to be followed in order to accept that offer without further communication from the seller, such as the goods are being sold on first come, first-served basis, such advertisement or catalogue description will be considered an offer [Rest. §26, Com. b]
5. Offer distinguished from Statements Made in Jest, in Anger, in a Grumbling Manner, or While Intoxicated
    - a. So long as an offeree *reasonably* believes that the offeror was manifesting an intention to be bound upon acceptance by the offeree, the fact that the offeror was only kidding, or was intoxicated, was grumbling, etc. does not prevent a valid offer from being made. See **Hawkins v. McGee**, *supra*

D. TYES OF OFFERS
   i. Offer to enter into a Unilateral Contract
      1. A unilateral contract offer is one in which the offeror is seeking *performance* of an act by the offeree as the acceptance. The offeror is **not** seeking the offeree's promise to perform an act, but instead is saying that he is offering to pay only on completion of a specified act
         a. Ex: I promise to pay you $1,000 if you actually paint my house
   ii. Offer to enter into a Bilateral Contract
      1. An offer to enter into a bilateral contract is one in which the offeror seeks a *promise of performance* by the offeree
         a. Ex: I promise to pay you $1,000 if you agree to paint my house by the end of the month
   iii. Significance of the distinction between unilateral and bilateral contract offers
      1. Most offers are bilateral in nature because of the concept of breach
      2. If an offeror says "I will only pay you if you paint my house," he cannot reasonably rely on the house being painted, because the offeree has not promised to start. On the other hand, if the offeree promises to paint the house by a certain date, the offeror has a right to expect that the work will be done, and if it is not, he will have a right to sue for breach of contract if there is no justifiable excuse for the painter's non-performance

- E. ***** **EXAM APPROACH TO OFFER ISSUES** *****
    - i. The typical way "offers" are tested in a Contracts exam is to give you several communications between the parties (multiple phone calls, letters, etc.), and then require you to identify which of these communications constituted the offer. To decide, recall that the key test is whether a **hypothetical reasonable person** in the position of the other party would believe the communication by the offeror signified an intention to be bound. In making that call, remember the rules distinguishing offers from other communications as a matter of law, and that the *subjective intent of the offeror is irrelevant*

III. OFFER AND ACCEPTANCE: ACCEPTANCE

- A. ACCEPTANCE: DEFINED AND DISCUSSED
    - i. An "acceptance" is a manifestation by the offeree that he is willing to be bound by the terms of the offer. Acceptance can be written, oral, or expressed by conduct. In a simple face-to-face negotiation, acceptance is the last communication that results in contract formation. To be valid under §50 of the Restatement, an acceptance must be made:
        1. By someone entitled to accept the offer
        2. Whose power of acceptance has not been terminated
        3. In a manner permitted under the contract
- B. EFFECT OF ACCEPTANCE
    - i. Assuming the existence of valid *consideration*, timely *acceptance* of a *valid offer* in a permissible way by an authorized offeree creates an enforceable *contract*. A valid acceptance cuts off the offeror's right to terminate the offer, and, of course, also cuts off the offeree's right to reject the offer
- C. TEST TO DETERMINE WHETHER ACCEPTANCE HAS TAKEN PLACE: THE OBJECTIVE THEORY OF CONTRACTS
    - i. Whether or not an offeree has accepted an offer will be judged under the **objective theory of** contracts. The test is whether, to a hypothetical reasonable person in the position of the offeror, the offeree has manifested a willingness to be bound by the terms of the offer. If so, an acceptance has been made
    - ii. A strange effect of the objective theory of contracts is that sometimes an offeree may accept an offer without even knowing its contents. That is, so long as the offeree at least knew that some sort of offer had been tendered (even if its exact terms are unknown), and as long as a reasonable person in the offeror's position would have believed an acceptance had been tendered, the acceptance will be valid
    - iii. Cross-Offers are identical offers that parties exchange in the mail. The exchange of cross-offers does not form a contract; neither

party has manifested a willingness to accept the offer of the other party
- D. WHO IS ENTITLED TO ACCEPT THE OFFER
    - i. When an offer is made to someone, the offeree is said to have a **power of acceptance**. The general rule is that **an offer may only be accepted by the person in whom it is reasonably apparent that the offeror intended to create the power of acceptance when the offer was made** [Rest. §§29, 52]
    - ii. When an offeror specifically limits who may accept the offer, such limitation will be effective, for the offeror is the "master of the offer"
    - iii. Who is an eligible offeree is judged by the objective theory of contracts
        1. If a reasonable person in the purported offeree's shoes would believe the offer was being made to him or her, that person has the power to accept it. *Hence, the subjective intention of the offeror as to whom the offer was intended is irrelevant*
    - iv. Power to accept is not transferable
        1. Exception: Right to accept under an option contract is transferable
- E. WHEN AN OFFER MAY BE ACCEPTED: DURATION OF THE POWER OF ACCEPTANCE
    - i. A purported acceptance of an offer after the power of acceptance under that offer has been terminated is invalid
    - ii. Once an offer has been terminated, the offeree has thereafter neither the power nor right to accept the offer, *and any purported acceptance by the offeree is really a counter-offer*
    - iii. Termination of an offer. **What terminates is not the offer, but rather the offeree's power to accept the offer**
    - iv. Acts and events that terminate an offeree's power of acceptance under revocable offers
        1. A revocable offer may be accepted so long as the power of acceptance under it has not been terminated [Rest. §35]
        2. A "revocable offer" is any offer that is not an "irrevocable: one. Since there are only 4 situations in which an offer will be deemed "irrevocable", most offers are "revocable"
        3. The term "revocable" offer is a legal shorthand for an offer that can be terminated upon the happening of 8 separate acts or events:
            a. **Rejection or counter-offer** by the offeree
            b. **Lapse of time**
            c. **Express or implied revocation**
            d. **Death or incapacity of the offeror**
            e. **Death or incapacity of the offeree**

f. **Death or destruction of a person or thing essential to the contract's performance**
g. **Supervening illegality**
h. **Non-occurrence of any condition of acceptance** under the terms of the offer

v. Termination of offers through rejection and counter-offer by the offeree
1. A **rejection** occurs upon any manifestation by the offeree that he does not accept the offer and is unwilling to be bound under its terms [Rest. §38]
2. A **counter-offer** is an offer made by the offeree to the original offeror relating to the same subject matter as the original proposal, but on *different terms* than those proposed in the original offer. It has the effect of **implicitly rejecting the original offer** (thereby terminating the power of the offeree to thereafter accept the original offer) and proposing a new one in its place [Rest. §39]
3. Rejections and counter-offers immediately cut off power of acceptance even if offer was to be held open [Rest. §38]
    a. Exception: When offer specifically states it will be kept open despite rejection or counter-offer [Rest. §39(2), Com. c]
4. Rejections and counter-offers are judged under the objective theory of contracts
5. Mere "Inquiries" or Preliminary Negotiations do not rise to the level of a counter-offer [Rest. §39, Com. b, Ill. 2]
6. Requests for Modification are not counter-offers
7. Intention to take the offer under further advisement does not terminate the power of acceptance
8. When a rejection is effective. The general rule is that a **rejection is effective upon receipt by the offeror**
9. When an acceptance is effective. The general rule is that **acceptances are effective upon dispatch** by the offeree

vi. Termination of Offers by Revocation
1. **Revocable offers can be freely rescinded by the offeror up until the moment of acceptance**. That is, so long as it has not been accepted, the offeror can "take back" an offer, even if he promised to keep it open
2. Revocations are judged under the objective theory of contracts
3. General Rule: To be effective, a revocation must be transmitted by the offeror to the offeree
    a. Exception: The indirect revocation doctrine
        i. The offeror must have taken a definite act inconsistent with an intention to enter into the proposed contract, AND

        ii. The offeree must have heard about the offeror's conduct from a reliable and trustworthy source [Rest. §43, Com. d]
- vii. Irrevocable Offers. The four situations in which an offer will be deemed "irrevocable"
    a. When the parties have entered into an **option contract**
    b. When a merchant fulfills the requirements of a **merchant's firm offer** in a UCC contract
    c. The temporary irrevocability that results under a **unilateral option contract** when the requirements of **Rest. §45** are met
    d. The temporary irrevocability that results from an **equitable option** when the offeree **substantially and foreseeably relies** on the offer under **Rest. §87(2) are met**
- viii. Option Contracts: Defined and Discussed
    1. An option contract is a special contract whose purpose is to define the length of time an offeree has to accept an offer to enter into an underlying agreement [Rest. §25]
    2. Effect of Option Contract: Elevating the Offeree's Power to Accept to the Offeree's *Right* to Accept
        a. An offeree with a contractual right to accept is entitled to assign the right to accept the offer, whereas an offeree with only a power to accept may not assign the power of acceptance to another
    3. Option Contracts and "Purported" Consideration
        a. Ordinarily a contract is not enforceable unless the party's promises are supported by consideration
        b. However, the Restatement makes an exception. As long as:
            i. The underlying deal is **fair**
            ii. The option contract is in **writing**, AND
            iii. The option contract is **signed by the offeror**, then the option contract is enforceable even if there is only "purported" or "recited" consideration, i.e., the option contract will be enforceable if the parties *merely state in their option contract that consideration was paid* even if no money actually changed hands [Rest. §87(1), Com. b]
- ix. Merchant's Firm Offer
    1. Under UCC §2-205, a merchant's offer may become irrevocable even in the absence of real or even purported consideration which would be necessary to establish an

option contract. For this to occur, the following must be established:
- a. The **offeror** (but not the *offeree*) must be a **merchant**, within the definition of UCC §2-104(1)
- b. The offer must be **in a writing signed by the merchant offeror**, AND
- c. The writing must **expressly state** that the **offer** is intended to be **irrevocable or will be held open**

2. If those three criteria are met, then the offer will be deemed irrevocable for the amount of time stated in the letter, or if no time is stated, for a reasonable period of time, *but in no event will the offer be deemed irrevocable for more than 3 months*

x. Making unilateral contracts temporarily irrevocable under Rest. §45
1. Once an offeree of a *unilateral* contract offer **begins performance**, a **unilateral option contract is implied** whereby the *offer becomes irrevocable for a reasonable period of time* in order to allow the offeree to complete performance
2. Problems associated with Rest. §45's approach in making a unilateral contract offer temporarily irrevocable
    - a. When does an offeree "begin performance"? This is ambiguous. The general idea is that the more specific acts the offeree can point out that were done to enable him to perform under the particular contract at issue, the more likely it is that performance has begun
    - b. Is it fair that the option contract is unilateral in effect, i.e., that it forces the offeror to leave open the offer, but it does not require the offeree to complete performance? There's no solution to this problem

xi. Making certain contract offers temporarily irrevocable by substantial reliance under Rest. §87(2). (**Equitable option** for the offeree)
1. Sometimes an offeree will substantially rely on an offer even before he accepts it. Such reliance may be shown by use of the offer in another presentation, by incurring substantial expense in anticipation of accepting the offer, etc. **An offer will be deemed irrevocable for a reasonable period of time if reliance on it is substantial and foreseeable enough**. The provision states that an **offeror's power to revoke is terminated** and an option contract is completed, whereby an **offer is deemed irrevocable** to the extent necessary to avoid injustice when:

a. An offeree takes action (or forbears to take action) of a *substantial nature* in response to an offer AND
b. Such action is *reasonably foreseeable* given the nature of the offer

2. Ex: ***Drennan v. Star Paving Co.*** Star Paving (offeror), a subcontractor, submitted a bid to Drennan (offeree), a general contractor, for paving work to be done on a large project. Drennan used Star Paving's bid in preparing its own quote for the entire project. Drennan was eventually awarded the contract to build the overall project by the developer. However, **before** Drennan could tell Star Paving its bid to do the paving work was **accepted**, Star Paving tried to revoke its bid. Notwithstanding the attempted revocation, Drennan went ahead and "accepted" anyway. Star Paving's argument was that normal contract rules provide that absent an option contract, a merchant's firm offer, or a situation under Rest. §45, **offers are freely revocable until accepted**, and Drennan had **not** accepted its offer before the revocation. Drennan, on the other hand, said it could hardly be expected to accept Star Paving's offer before it knew whether it was awarded the contract to build the entire project by the developer, for unless it had such contract, it would have no use for Star Paving's services. Held: Drennan prevailed under Rest. §87(2)

xii. Acts and Events that Terminate the Power of Acceptance Even Under Irrevocable Offers:
1. Upon the **expiration of a reasonable time** or the *time specified for acceptance*:
    a. In an *option contract* OR
    b. In a *merchant's firm offer*
2. The **supervening destruction or death of a thing essential for performance**
3. **The non-occurrence of a condition, the occurrence of which is necessary to accept the offer** (usually specified in the option contract or merchant's firm offer)
4. Under the *majority rule,* **rejection or counter-offer by the offeree,** *followed by reasonable, foreseeable, and detrimental reliance by the offeror* [Rest. §37]
    a. Ex: Under a valid option contract, Jimmy has 30 days from January 15 to purchase Tommy's car for $5,000. On January 17, Jimmy tells Tommy "There's no way I'm going to exercise my option and buy your car for $5,000. If you take $3,500 for it now, I'd buy it." If Tommy does nothing, Jimmy still has until February 14 to purchase the car because rejections and counter-offers, per *se*, do not

terminate the offeree's power of acceptance under an irrevocable offer. However, if Tommy had then sold the car to Billy, Jimmy's power and right to accept, even though the subject of an irrevocable offer, has terminated due to Jimmy's rejection and Tommy's subsequent reasonable, foreseeable, and detrimental reliance on the rejection in selling the car to Billy

    xiii. Accordingly, the following acts or events, which will terminate the power of acceptance under revocable offers, **do *not* terminate the power of acceptance under irrevocable offers**:
1. Rejection and counter-offer by the offeree, NOT followed by detrimental reliance on the part of the offeror
2. Attempted revocation by the offeror
3. Death or incapacity by the offeror
4. Death or incapacity of the offeree

F. HOW AN OFFER MAY BE ACCEPTED: PERMISSIBLE METHODS OR MODES OF ACCEPTANCE
    i. As master of the offer, the offeror can set forth which of the only four possible ways an offer may be accepted
1. By requiring the offeree to **promise to perform** the action requested in the offer
2. By requiring the offeree to **actually perform** the action requested in the offer
3. By requiring the offeree to **begin to perform** the action requested in the offer OR
4. In certain cases, by **silence and/or inaction** of the offeree

    ii. General rules regarding acceptance of an offer which does not specify explicitly the method of acceptance
1. If an offer does not specify how it is to be accepted, it may be accepted in any manner and by any medium *reasonable* under the circumstances [Rest. §30(2)]

G. Posting Problems: The Mailbox Rule
    i. General rules
1. **Offers, revocations, and rejections are effective on *receipt***
2. **Acceptances are effective on *dispatch***
    a. A properly dispatched acceptance will be effective, **even if it never gets to the offeror**
    b. Exception: Unless explicitly provided to the contrary, **acceptance of the underlying offer that is the subject of an option contract is not effective until it is received by the offeror**
3. Effect of first sending a rejection, followed by an acceptance. **The acceptance is effective if it arrives first, and the rejection is effective if it arrives first**

4. Effect of first sending an acceptance, followed by a rejection
   a. **The acceptance is effective on dispatch unless:**
      i. **The rejection arrives first AND**
      ii. **The offeror changes his position in reliance on the rejection**

H. ***** <u>EXAM APPROACH TO ACCEPTANCE ISSUES</u> *****
   i. Make sure the offer is still open when it is purportedly accepted, i.e., determine whether the offer is revocable or irrevocable, and whether any act or event has occurred that will terminate the offeree's power or right to accept
   ii. Make sure the party who accepts the offer has a valid power of acceptance, meaning the offeror gave the party a power of acceptance when making the offer, or that the accepting party has been assigned the right to accept under a valid option contract by a proper offeree
   iii. Make sure the offer is accepted by a proper method of acceptance, i.e, one that is either specified in the offer, or is reasonable under the circumstances
   iv. Make sure the acceptance is timely, either in light of the time specified for acceptance in the offer, or a reasonable time if no time is mentioned, always keeping in mind the mail box rules regarding the effectiveness of various communications
   v. Lastly, keep in mind that acceptances are judged under the objective theory of contracts, so that intent of the accepting party is irrelevant, and watch out for the special problems associated with specific issues such as cross-offers and general or reward offers

IV. **OFFER AND ACCEPTANCE: WHEN THE "ACCEPTANCE" VARIES FROM THE OFFER: THE MIRROR IMAGE RULE AND UCC §2-207 ("BATTLE OF THE FORMS")**

   A. COMMON LAW VIEW: THE MIRROR IMAGE RULE
      i. Under C/L, an effective acceptance had to accept the offer *unconditionally* and entirely. If the purported acceptance added an additional term, had one fewer term, or even slightly changed a term, it was considered a counter-offer not an acceptance
   B. UNFAIRNESS OF MIRROR IMAGE RULE
      i. The mirror image rule makes sense in face-to-face transactions
      ii. In modern commercial transactions, where offer and acceptance are often made via pre-printed forms, the mirror image rule often leads to unfairness. There are two ways the unfairness comes about:
         1. Unfairness where one party doesn't perform

a. Ex: Kendall, a farmer in Kansas, sends a "purchase order" form to a grain supplier in Ohio. Clause 36 of his purchase order is pre-printed and states that UPS shall make delivery. Upon receiving the purchase order, the grain supplier sends out a preprinted form entitled "acceptance of purchase order". Clause 31 of the acceptance is pre-printed and says that delivery is to be made by any common carrier. When the acceptance form arrives, Kendall checks only to ensure that the quantity, price, and delivery dates are correct, and puts the document in his files. If the grain company never delivers the corn, under the mirror-image rule there is no breach of contract because no contract was ever formed. Because of the discrepancies in the delivery term (UPS vs. any common carrier) the "acceptance" was only a counter-offer which was itself never accepted
 2. Unfairness where the parties perform: the "Last Shot" doctrine
    a. Ex: Tony Montana places an order for 1000 kilos of Columbian cocaine from Mr. Ortiz. On the purchase order Tony uses to order the cocaine is the clause "supplier warrants that all cocaine supplied under this contract shall be of snortable quality." Ortiz sends back an acknowledgment form that is identical to the purchase order in every respect, except that his form states "supplier represents its products are only of injectable, not snortable, quality." Neither party looks at the other's form and the cocaine is delivered and paid for. Later, when the cocaine turns out to be un-snortable, Tony sues Ortiz. **Under the mirror image rule, the parties never had a contract based on the exchange of forms.** Further, Ortiz's form was the pending offer at the time the parties performed, C/L held that when Tony paid for the coke, **he implicitly accepted Ortiz's counter-offer**, and thus became bound to a contract whose terms included the injectable only quality warranty. This rule is called the "last shot" doctrine and resulted in a contract by performance being made on the terms of the last party to submit a form

C. UCC §2-207: AN OVERVIEW
   i. §2-207 of the UCC is intended to eliminate the unfairness of C/L view

ii. It does do by eliminating the mirror-image rule and last shot doctrine, and allowing for a valid acceptance to contain terms different from or additional to an offer
iii. Not only does §2-207 govern whether the parties have a contract (i.e., whether there was an offer and an acceptance), but it also determines what **the terms** of that resulting contract are. It is only in this latter capacity that §2-207 becomes complicated

D. ANALYSIS OF §2-207 PROBLEMS
  i. After ascertaining that the rules of Article 2 of the UCC govern the transaction, nearly all §2-207 problems can be analyzed in only three steps
    1. **Do the parties have a contract based on the exchange of their writings under §2-207(1)?** (i.e., is the purported acceptance actually an effective acceptance, or is it a counter-offer as would be true under common law?)
    2. **If the offeree's form is an effective acceptance, then the terms of the contract are dictated by the rules of §2-207(2)**
    3. **If the offeree's form is not an effective acceptance, then the parties do not have a contract based on their writings under §2-207(1). In that case it is necessary to examine whether they have a contract by conduct under §2-207(3), and if they do, to use §2-207(3) to determine the terms of that contract**
  ii. First Step: Do the parties have a contract based on their writings under §2-207(1)? (Example for discussion here: The offeror is a buyer who orders a product on a Purchase Order form, and the offeree is a seller who purports to accept that order by an Acknowledgment form which differs from the Purchase Order in some respect)
    1. **The only function of §2-207(1) is to determine if the Purchase Order and Acknowledgment together constitute a binding offer and acceptance.** This is done in two sub-steps:
      a. **Determining whether the seller/offeree's Acknowledgment is a "seasonable expression of acceptance"**
        i. If the purported acceptance is too different from the offer, it is **not** an acceptance, but will be deemed a counter-offer, and the determination of whether the parties have a contract is judged under §2-207(3) not §2-207(1). In other words, §2-207(1) will allow a purported acceptance to be an effective acceptance even if it contains different or additional terms from the offer, but when

16

either the *number of differences* between the seller's and buyer's form gets too great, or when the seller's form *differs sufficiently in an essential term* (quality, price, quantity) from that found in the purchase order, the acknowledgment will be deemed a counter-offer, not an acceptance

b. **Ascertaining whether the seller's acceptance is "expressly made conditional" on the buyer/offeror's assent to [any] different or additional terms**
   i. §2-207(1) provides that if the seller's form makes acceptance expressly conditional on assent to the additional or different terms found in seller's form, then the Acknowledgment will be treated as a counter-offer and not an acceptance
   ii. To be an effective counter-offer under §2-207(1), the offeree-seller's form must clearly communicate both:
      1. **That the seller is unwilling to go forward on the terms of the offer AND**
      2. **that its own terms will not control unless the buyer-offeror EXPRESSLY, not implicitly, assents to the seller's different or additional terms**
         a. This eliminates the C/L last shot doctrine
         b. Express assent means the buyer's **specific affirmative assent** is required
         c. Ex: *C. Itoh & Co. v. Jordon International*. The seller's form stated that its acceptance was "expressly conditional on Buyer's assent to the additional terms and conditions set forth below." The court held that the above language was sufficient to turn the purported acceptance into a counter-offer, and thus the parties had no contract based on the exchange of

17

writings. Whether they had a contract at all was thus determined by §2-207(3)
            d. Without "expressly conditional on buyer's specific affirmative assent" language, the seller's form will become a valid acceptance, not a counter-offer, and §2-207(2) then governs
        iii. Second Step: If the parties have a contract based on their exchanged writings under §2-207(1), then §2-207(2) governs what *terms* make up the contract
            1. If either party is a non-merchant, the offeror's terms control
                a. Any additional terms contained in the acceptance are merely proposals for addition to the contract, which may be accepted or not by the offeror
            2. If both parties are merchants, offeree's terms control *unless* one of the following three §2-207(2) exceptions apply:
                a. The **offer expressly limits acceptance to the terms of the offer**
                b. The additional terms in the acceptance **materially alter** the offer (these are terms negating warranties, requiring standards above normal trade standards, unreasonable time limits, indemnity provisions)
                c. **Notification of objection** to the additional terms by the offeror is given within a reasonable time after notice of them has been received
            3. Thus, only if **none** of these three conditions apply will the additional terms become part of the contract. It is very rare that such will be the case, **so the probable result under §2-207(2), even with merchants, is that the offeror's terms will still control the deed**
        iv. Third Step: If no contract is formed under §2-207(1) based on the exchanged writings, an implied-in-fact contract may be formed on the parties' conduct under §2-207(3). If so, the "Knockout Rule" of §2-207(3) will determine which *terms* become part of the contract
            1. §2-207(2) plays absolutely no role in this situation since its only function is to provide the rules for determining what terms are part of the contract **if** a contract is made by exchange of the writings under §2-207(1)
            2. §2-207(3) provides that even if the offeree is deemed to have sent a counter-offer that is never formally accepted, the parties can establish an implied-in-fact contract by their conduct. Thus, if the seller sends the goods called for in the

offer, and the buyer accepts them, they have made a contract by conduct under §2-207(3)
3. If the parties do have a contract based on the exchange of their writings, its terms **must** be governed by §2-207(2). In other words, resort to §2-207(3) can only be made when **no** contract is formed based on the parties' exchanged writings as judged by application of the rules in §2-207(1)
4. The "Knock-Out" Rule
    a. The **terms** of the contract consist of those **terms** on which the writings of the **parties agree, together with any supplementary terms** incorporated under any other provision of the UCC
    b. Thus, all the terms which are in both parties writings become part of the contract, but any term that is not found in **both** documents is "knocked out" and does not become part of the contract
    c. If at the end of the "knock-out" process the contract is left with no terms regarding price, time of delivery, place of delivery, time of payment, or place of payment, such terms can be supplied by the UCC's gap fillers which are some of the supplementary terms referred to in §2-207(3)
v. When the additional or different terms are found in a confirmation instead of an acceptance
    1. There is no need to inquire whether the parties have entered into a contract based on their exchanged writings under §2-207(1), since by definition a "confirmation" confirms that a contract exists, and merely serves to restate the terms of the contract
    2. Analysis proceeds directly to §2-207(2) to determine the terms of the contract
    3. To analogize a "confirmation" situation to a more typical §2-207 analysis with exchanged writings by both parties, think of the oral contract as the "offer" and the written confirmation as the "acceptance" under §2-207(2)
E. ***** <u>**EXAM APPROACH TO §2-207 ISSUES**</u> *****
    i. Determine whether the purported acceptance is truly an acceptance under §2-207(1) despite the presence of additional or different terms, or is it a counter-offer (usually because it contains a clause, e.g., "this acceptance expressly conditioned on Buyer's assent to any additional or different terms")
    ii. If the purported acceptance is deemed a valid acceptance, then the terms of the contract are determined under §2-207(2) (and §2-207(3) is never used)
    iii. If the purported acceptance is found not to be a valid acceptance, the parties have no contract based on their exchanged writings (and

§2-207(2) is never used). However, if the parties perform they have a contract by conduct, and the rules of §2-207(3) determine that contract's terms

V. CONSIDERATION AND ITS "SUBSTITUTES": CONSIDERATION

A. THE CONSIDERATION DOCTRINE
  i. Think of consideration as "payment" for a promise. That is, for a promise from a promisor to be valid, the promisee has to "pay for it" in some way
  ii. If an agreement is not supported by valid consideration, that agreement is not an enforceable contract
  iii. However, *certain promises* in an otherwise unenforceable agreement may be enforced under a promissory estoppel theory
B. DEFINITIONS OF CONSIDERATION
  i. While the concepts contained in the various definitions are important and need to be learned, you should keep in mind that no one theory completely describes all the contours of the consideration doctrine
   1. The "Benefit/Detriment" Theory
      a. A promise is deemed supported by consideration (and thus enforceable), whenever:
         i. The promisee either acts, or promises to act, **in exchange for the promisor's promise**, AND
         ii. The promisee's act or promised act is *either* a **legal detriment to the promisee** *or* a **legal benefit to the promisor**
            1. Ex: Unilateral Contract. Benny makes an offer to enter into a unilateral contract with Sean, promising to pay him $1,000 for his watch. If Sean gives Benny his watch in exchange for his promise to pay the $1,000 (thereby accepting the offer), Benny's promise to pay the $1,000 is enforceable under the benefit/detriment theory. That is Sean, the promisee, suffered a **legal detriment** (he gave up possession of his watch), and Benny, the promisor, received a **legal benefit** (he obtained possession of the watch). Further, Sean's detriment was given **in exchange for Benny's promise** to

pay the $1,000. Thus, the parties have entered into a valid, enforceable unilateral contract with a promissory offer, an acceptance by conduct, and consideration to enforce Benny's promise to pay
              2. Ex: Bilateral Contract. Sean promises to give Benny his watch at a later time in return for Benny's promise to pay $1,000 for it. Benny's promise to pay is enforceable, Sean suffered a **legal detriment** (he promised to give up possession of the watch), and Benny received a **legal benefit** (he was promised possession of the watch) **in exchange for his promise** of the $1,000 payment. Note also that Sean's promise to give up the watch (i.e., his promissory acceptance) is also enforceable. Benny received a legal detriment (he promised to pay $1,000), Sean obtained a legal benefit (receipt of Benny's promise to pay), **in exchange for Sean's** promise to give up the watch. As such, the parties have entered into a valid, enforceable bilateral contract, with a promissory offer, a promissory acceptance, and consideration to support the executory promises
    2. The Restatement's "Bargain Theory"
        a. The Restatement rejected the benefit/detriment theory in favor of the "bargain" theory
        b. Under the restatement approach "to constitute consideration, a performance or return promise must be bargained for" [Rest. §71(1)]
        c. [Rest. §71(2)] A performance is **bargained for** if:
            i. it is **sought by** the promisor in exchange for his promise AND
            ii. it is **given by the promisee in exchange for that promise**
                1. Ex: Unilateral Contract. (Assume the same facts in the Benny/Sean transaction as set forth in the above

unilateral contract example). Benny's promise to pay the $1,000 is enforceable under the bargain theory. That is, Sean's act in giving up the watch was "bargained for" because it was both **sought by** Benny (the promisor) and given by Sean (the promisee), **in exchange for** Benny's promise to pay. Thus, the parties entered into a valid enforceable unilateral contract, with a promissory offer, an acceptance by conduct, and consideration sufficient to enforce Benny's executory promise

2. Ex: Bilateral Contract. (Assume the same facts in the Benny/Sean transaction as set forth in the above Bilateral contract example). Benny's promise to pay the $1,000 is enforceable, for Sean's promised performance (his promise to give the watch at a later time), was "bargained for", i.e., it was **sought by** Benny, and **given in exchange for** Benny's promise to pay. Similarly, Sean's promise to give the watch is enforceable, for Benny's performance (his promise to pay $1,000) was **sought by Sean**, and **given in exchange** for his promise to deliver the watch. Thus, the parties entered into a valid, enforceable bilateral contract, with a promissory offer, a promissory acceptance, and consideration sufficient to enforce the executory promises

3. Modern contract law's acceptance of the benefit/detriment and bargain theories of consideration
    a. Courts tend to cite both views of consideration today
    b. Some courts have combined both tests, stating that consideration is present only when there has been a benefit/ and or detriment that was **bargained for**, rather than merely given "in exchange" as required by the earlier test

22

C. TYPES OF CONSIDERATION IN UNILATERAL CONTRACTS
  i. In a unilateral contract, the consideration supporting the offeror's promise consists of one of the following bargained for elements:
     1. An **act**
     2. A **forbearance**, OR
     3. The **creation, modification, or destruction of a legal relationship** [Rest. §71(2), (3)]
  ii. To be considered a valid consideration to support the enforceability of the promises made in a unilateral contract, one of these three elements must be **sought by** the promisor and undertaken by the promisee in exchange for the promise made in the offer
     1. Ex: ***Hamer v. Sidway***. Uncle offers to pay 16 year-old nephew $1,000 if nephew refrains from smoking and drinking until age 21. If nephew does not smoke and drink until age 21, the uncle's promise to pay is supported by consideration (and thus enforceable), for nephew undertook a **forbearance in exchange** for uncle's promise, and that forbearance was **sought by** Uncle when he made his offer
D. TYPES OF CONSIDERATION IN BILATERAL CONTRACTS
  i. In a bilateral contract, **each party's promise serves as consideration for the return promise of the other** if, but only IF:
     1. Each promise was **sought by**, and was given **in exchange for** the other, AND
     2. The performance promised by each party would be valid consideration if it were carried out [Rest. §75]
E. THE RETURN PROMISES OR PERFORMANCES BY THE PROMISEE CAN BE VALID CONSIDERATION EVEN IF GIVEN TO A THIRD PARTY
F. TRANSACTIONS WITHOUT CONSIDERATION BECAUSE THEY LACK A BARGAINED FOR EXCHANGE
  i. There are two types of promises or actions which historically have been deemed insufficient to provide consideration for a contract, for they lack the "bargained for exchange" element
     1. Gifts or gift promises
     2. Unsolicited actions
  ii. Traditional Rule: Gift promises are Unenforceable because they are not supported by consideration
     1. Acts "Incidental" to a true gift promise are insufficient consideration to enforce the promise
        a. The key inquiry is whether the promisor made the promise in order to "get something" from the exchange or does the act called for merely make more convenient the giving of a gift
           i. Ex: ***Kirksey v. Kirksey***. Relative wrote to recently widowed sister-in-law, "If you

come down and see me, I will let you have a place to raise your family." Sister-in-law moved to Alabama with her family, but brother-in-law would not provide her a place to live when she arrived. **Held**: The offer of a place to live was only a gift promise, and thus the actions requested of sister-in-law were merely *incidental* to the true nature of the offer. Note that the sister-in-law could recover at least the expenses for her trip to Alabama, and perhaps more, under a theory of *promissory estoppel*

G. SPECIFIC TYPES OF TRANSACTIONS RAISING CONSIDERATION ISSUES
   i. There are certain types of transactions whose very natures raise consideration issues. The overriding principle is that as long as the promises or performances of one party are both sought by the other in making a promise, and are given in exchange for that promise, consideration is probably present
      1. Transactions in which the consideration of one party is worth substantially less than the other: the "dollar" theory of consideration
         a. Typically, courts will not inquire into the adequacy of one party's consideration, even if its economic value seems disproportionate to the economic value of the other party's [Rest. §79]
         b. Thus, at C/L a dollar can generally serve as valid consideration for any promise, no matter how extravagant, so long as the promise was freely bargained for and freely given in exchange for the dollar
         c. Inadequate consideration may be evidence of fraud, duress, or undue influence
            i. While a court will not void a contract based solely on the adequacy of consideration, a disproportionate economic benefit realized by one party may serve as circumstantial evidence of the existence of a doctrine that would allow one party to void the contract, and entitles the court to examine the transaction carefully to ensure that the promises of the parties were freely and voluntarily bargained for
         d. Inadequate consideration may be evidence of sham consideration

- i. Ex: Uncle Teddy wants to give his niece his $136,000 Mercedes Benz S600 with GPS. Knowing gift promises to be unenforceable, Teddy agrees to "sell" the Benz to niece now for $1, with delivery in two years. If the "bargain" is only a pretense to disguise a gift promise, niece's payment of $1 is not consideration for Teddy's promise to deliver the car. Hence, inadequate consideration may also serve as evidence of a sham transaction which is unenforceable under contract law
2. Illusory Promises
    a. An illusory promise is one in which the promisor gives the illusion of making a valid promise to act or forebear, but in reality does not bind himself or herself to do anything. **A true illusory promise cannot serve as consideration**
    b. Ex: If in response to an offer to purchase a couch for $500, Bill responds, "I promise to pay you $500 for the couch if I decide I want to, otherwise I will not take the couch and will pay you nothing." Bill has made no real commitment, and thus no enforceable contract is formed
    c. Traditional Rule: Unless a definite commitment was evident, a promise lacked consideration: personal satisfaction clauses
        i. The C/L rule was clear: **a contract with a personal satisfaction clause was illusory because the promisor failed to make a definite commitment to be bound, the promise was illusory** and thus insufficient to act as consideration
    d. Modern Rule: The implied duty of good faith and fair dealing renders personal satisfaction clauses enforceable
        i. ***Any* restriction on a promisor's freedom of action, whether express or implied, will prevent a promise from being classified as illusory**
        ii. One of the implied restrictions on a promisor's freedom of action is **an implied duty of good faith ("honesty") in performance**. That is, in **every contract**, the parties will be deemed to have agreed to

perform under the contract in good faith. [Rest. §205, UCC §1-203]
e. Special illusory promise problems regarding Termination-At-Will Clauses
    i. Traditional Rule: Contracts with Termination-At-Will Clauses are illusory and hence unenforceable
    ii. Modern Rule: Contracts with Termination-At-Will clauses probably enforceable
        1. Most courts hold that a termination-at-will clause requires the party terminating the contract to give reasonable notice to the other. The fact that the terminating party must give notice is a sufficient detriment, i.e., a sufficient restriction on the promisor's actions, so as to render the promise enforceable. In other words, the requirement that the **promisee give notice** is a sufficient bargained for restriction on the promisee's actions to constitute consideration
    iii. The UCC approach to Terminable-At-Will contracts: the reasonable notification requirement avoids illusory promise issues
        1. Under UCC §2-309(3), in order to terminate a contract validly, termination must take place either upon the happening of an agreed event or after reasonable notification is received
    iv. Employment Terminable-At-Will
        1. In employment contracts if no duration term is provided, most courts have held that either party may terminate at-will even if the parties have set the compensation at a specified sum per month, day, or year
        2. Frequently an employer states that the employment will be "permanent." Most courts have thought that this term simply means that the employment is foreseen as steady rather than seasonal or for a

particular project; thus, the employment is at-will
3. According to a minority view, however, if permanent employment is promised, the employee is entitled to work so long as the employee is able to do the work and the employer continues in the business for which the employee is hired
4. Even under the majority view, some courts have held that the hiring is not at-will if a consideration over and above the consideration supplied by the employee's services or promises of services is exchanged for the promise of permanent employment
5. Courts may not enforce at-will contracts if the discharge is contrary to public policy. A New Hampshire court stated in ***Monge v. Beebe Rubber Co***. "We hold that a termination by the employer of a contract of employment at will which is motivated by bad faith or malice or based on retaliation is not in the best interest of the economic system or the public good and constitutes a breach of the employment contract"
6. Courts try to fit employment contracts so that they fall outside of the *statute of frauds*

3. Purported, but unperformed, consideration is not effective consideration
    a. Purported consideration is consideration that is intended to have taken place in exchange for a promise, but which in fact never occurred
    b. Ex: A signed document may say "For $500 received from Reggie, I hereby sell to him my antique desk" If the $500 is never actually paid, the seller can sue Reggie for breach, regardless of the fact that the "contract" says the $500 was paid. Similarly, if the $500 is never paid, Reggie cannot seek to enforce the seller to deliver the desk because purported consideration is not sufficient to make a promise enforceable

i. Exception: Purported consideration is sufficient for option contracts
    1. [Rest. §87, Com. c] Purported consideration is sufficient to make effective the promises made in an option contract, as long as the offer for the option contract is in writing, signed by the offeror, and proposes a fair exchange
        a. Ex: If a written option contract recites that for $20 received, Pauly gives Danny an option to purchase his car for $50,000 within 30 days, Pauly is obligated to sell the car to Danny if he tenders the $50,000 within 30 days, even if Danny never paid the original $20

H. ***** **EXAM APPROACH TO CONSIDERATION ISSUES** *****
  i. Where consideration is an issue, make sure you analyze:
      1. Whether the promise involved was **bargained for**, i.e., was sought by the promisor in exchange for his promise and given by the promisee in exchange for that promise, AND
      2. Whether, as a result of the bargain, **the relevant party or parties suffered** a legal detriment, i.e., he became obligated to do something that he was not obligated to do before the agreement
  ii. If you determine that the promise involved cannot meet the above test, then determine whether one of the modern "exceptions" to the consideration requirements are present:
      1. The implication of "good faith" to save output, requirements, and exclusive dealing contracts, and contracts with "personal satisfaction" clauses
      2. A gift promise for past benefits made enforceable via Rest. §86
      3. A promise to pay a debt otherwise unenforceable because of the statute of limitations or bankruptcy
      4. The implication of a "notice" requirement to save termination-at-will clauses
  iii. If the promise is not supportable by either the bargain/legal detriment theory, or by one of the modern exceptions to the rule, then classify it properly as a promise that is unenforceable due to:
      1. The gift promise rules
      2. The past or moral consideration doctrine
      3. The unsolicited actions rules

28

4. The illusory promise doctrine
5. The pre-existing duty rule
6. The sham consideration doctrine
7. The purported consideration rule

VI. CONSIDERATION AND ITS SUBSTITUTES: PROMISSORY ESTOPPEL

A. THE PROMISSORY ESTOPPEL DOCTRINE
   i. The doctrine of promissory estoppel is based on the premise that where the promises of one party have led the other to justifiably and reasonably rely on those promises being carried out, the promises should be enforced **even if they were only gratuitous, or not otherwise supported by consideration**
   ii. In essence, the doctrine estops (prevents) a party from denying reasonable obligations *foreseeably* resulting from *reliance* on his promise, and estops a party from being able to deny liability on the technical ground that no "bargained for exchange" resulted upon the acceptance of an offer

B. PROMISSORY ESTOPPEL IS NOT A "SUBSTITUTE" FOR CONSIDERATION
   i. Recovery under a promissory estoppel theory is not a recovery based on "contract." Rather, it is a recovery based on a mixture of equitable and tort law principles
   ii. Promises governed by promissory estoppel are only enforceable to the extent that "justice requires", which may fall short of full enforceability
   iii. Promissory estoppel does more than make enforceable gratuitous promises exchanged as "offers" and "acceptances"
      1. It makes some offers irrevocable
      2. It enforces some promises made during preliminary negotiations which do not rise to the level of offers
   iv. Promissory estoppel only applies to certain *promises*. It does not "step in" and automatically make an entire *contract* enforceable. **If it applies, only the promises in the agreement that were actually relied upon become enforceable**

C. ELEMENTS OF PROMISSORY ESTOPPEL UNDER THE RESTATEMENT
   i. Rest. §90 states that a **promise is binding if**:
      1. **In making the promise the promisor should *reasonably* expect to induce action or forbearance (*reliance*) on the part of the promisee**
      2. **The promise does in fact induce *foreseeable* action or forbearance (*reliance*) by the promisee, AND**
      3. ***Injustice* can be avoided only by enforcement of the promise**

ii. If these criteria are met, the promise may be enforced, but only to the extent "justice requires"
iii. Ex: ***Ricketts v. Scothorn***. Grandfather is upset to find granddaughter working and gives her a $2,000 promissory note, redeemable on demand, telling her the note will see to it that she will never have to work again. Granddaughter quits work immediately, but did not attempt to redeem promissory note until several years later, after grandfather had died. His executors refused to pay. **Held**: The promise to pay the $2,000 is enforceable under a promissory estoppel theory. The promise could not be upheld under a consideration theory since it was clearly a gift. However, because it **was** a promise that (1) reasonably could be expected to induce action on the part of the granddaughter in reliance on it (quitting her job); (2) actually did induce such action (she did quit); and (3) would be unjust not to enforce under the circumstances, the promise was enforceable under promissory estoppel to the extent justice requires. In this case, justice required full enforcement of the promise

D. TYPES OF PROMISES ENFORCEABLE UNDER PROMISSORY ESTOPPEL
   i. Gift promises
   ii. Oral promises to convey land
       1. Ex: If Chad makes an un-bargained for, oral promise to convey Blackacre to Doug, and Doug relies on the promise by moving onto the land, making improvements, etc. and Doug is reasonable in believing he is entitled to make these improvements, most courts will hold the promise to convey is binding against Chad under a promissory estoppel theory [Rest. §§90, 139]. Whether Doug will get specific performance of the promise or simply be recompensed for his work on the land will depend on what "justice requires" given all the circumstances. Note that in this type of case the promissory estoppel doctrine not only overcomes a "no consideration" defense, but also overcomes a *Statute of Frauds* defense as well, thereby making enforceable an oral promise to convey an interest in land
   iii. Charitable Subscriptions
       1. [Rest. §90(2)]. **A pledge to a charity is enforceable even without proof that the promise induced any reliance whatsoever by the organization**
   iv. Offers that induce foreseeable reliance of a substantial nature become binding as option contracts to the extent necessary to avoid injustice
       1. [Rest. §87(2)]. Promissory estoppel will also serve to make any other type of offer irrevocable as an option contract (at least to the extent necessary to avoid injustice) if:

- a. **The offeror should reasonably and foreseeably expect the offeree to undertake substantial action in reliance on the offer**, AND
- b. **The offer actually does induce that reliance**
    - i. Ex: Food Co. makes an offer to Leu promising him that it is willing to buy all the carrots Leu grows this season at a fixed price. Food Co. tells Leu he may think about the offer for a month and need not accept before then. Leu immediately purchases carrot seed and informs Food Co. of his actions. Within two weeks Leu has dedicated a substantial portion of his farm to growing carrots. At this point, Food Co.'s offer is irrevocable until the end of the month, since Food Co. should reasonably have expected Leu to rely on the offer to a substantial degree, and because Leu has, in fact, relied on Food Co.'s promise

v. Offers by Subcontractors (formation problems)
  1. A general contractor will not accept the subcontractor's bid until the developer has accepted the general's bid to develop the entire project
  2. Under normal formation rules, an offer such as the one made by the sub is freely revocable until the time of acceptance
  3. However, under Rest. §87(2), **promissory estoppel makes the promisor's (ie., the subcontractor's) offer irrevocable until the general contractor has a reasonable chance to accept**
  4. Typically, that "reasonable time" extends to a day or two after the developer has awarded the bid to the general
  5. Ex: See ***Drennan v. Star Paving***, *supra*

vi. Actions taken in reliance on promises made in preliminary negotiations
  1. Some courts (although certainly not all) have held that a rather vague promise, of the type typically found in preliminary negotiations, may be enforceable to some extent if reliance on that promise was both foreseeable and reasonable
  2. Ex: ***Hoffman v. Red Owl Stores***. Red Owl franchises supermarkets. Its representative promised Hoffman that he would be awarded a franchise if he gained the necessary experience and invested $18,000. Hoffman started a two year quest to gain the necessary experience by quitting his then-present job, moving to another city to go to work in

another grocery store, borrowing $18,000 from a relative, etc. At the end of the two years, Red Owl stated the $18,000 franchise could not be paid with borrowed money and refused to award Hoffman a franchise. **Held**: No contract existed under the indefiniteness doctrine because there were simply too many details left open as to the terms of the proposed franchise to call it an offer, e.g. where the store was to be located, how soon he could operate it, etc. At most, the promise was part of a preliminary negotiation. Nevertheless, because Red Owl should have foreseen Hoffman would have relied on the promise to his detriment, and because Hoffman did in fact rely on the promise, it would now be unjust not to enforce the promise to some degree. Thus, under a promissory estoppel theory, Hoffman could recover the out of pocket costs he spent in reliance on the promise

3. Note that this case also sets forth the rather controversial doctrine that the parties owe a duty of good faith to each other not only in the performance and enforcement of the contract, but also during its **negotiation**. The case extends the obligation of good faith set forth in Rest. §205 and UCC §1-203

E. REMEDIES WHEN A PROMISE IS ENFORCED UNDER PROMISSORY ESTOPPEL
   i. Usually, the promisee is entitled to recover his full expectation interest, but where the *expectation* interest is greatly disproportionate to the promisee's actual reliance, or where the circumstances make it unjust (or impossible) to award the complete expectation interest, a promisee is only entitled to his or her *reliance* damages

F. ****EXAM APPROACH TO PROMISSORY ESTOPPEL ISSUES ****
   i. So you want to know how your contracts professor will test you on promissory estoppel issues, eh? Well, look no further, this little passage will enlighten you and lift your mind from the ignorance that it is wallowing in now
   ii. Most professors are wary of students relying too heavily on promissory estoppel to enforce promises, and thereby relying too little on the intricacies of consideration when writing exam answers. In theory, many (if not most) of the promises supported by consideration could just as easily be supported by promissory estoppel, i.e., most of the time, in a contract supported by consideration, it is reasonable to foresee that a bargained for promise will be relied upon by the other party, and usually it is actually relied upon as well. Given such action, it typically would be unjust not to enforce promises. However, as Justice Holmes

once said "a pervasive use of promissory estoppel would cut up the doctrine of consideration by the roots"
iii. Accordingly, in your analysis of formation issues, you should **first** determine whether a promise can be supported by consideration. If it can, your analysis should proceed from there. It is only when the promise cannot meet the requirements of consideration that you should examine whether the promise can be enforced by promissory estoppel

VII. VOIDABILITY, A FANCY NAME FOR CONTRACT DEFENSES: STATUTE OF FRAUDS

A. THE STATUTE OF FRAUDS DOCTRINE
  i. Purposes of the statute. By requiring a signed writing in order to make a contract enforceable, the statute of frauds is said to serve several purposes:
    1. To provide **evidence that the parties truly entered into a contract**
    2. To provide **a written record of what they agreed to**, rather than having to trust the memories of the parties as to what the terms of the contract were, AND
    3. To make unsophisticated parties aware that they are entering into an **agreement with legal ramifications**, i.e., when a party has to "sign" something it appears more formal, and thus more significant, than just making an oral promise
  ii. Effect of statute applying
    1. The fact that the statute is satisfied does **not** mean that, somehow, a contract is formed where one never existed. All it means is that a single defense – the defense of the Statute of Frauds – is unavailable in that action
B. CONTRACTS WHICH BY THEIR TERMS, CANNOT BE PERFORMED WITHIN A YEAR OF THEIR MAKING
  i. This is the only type of contract affected by the statute of frauds that most Prof's will cover in class. There are lots of other types of contracts the SOF governs.
  ii. The general rule is that if even a single promise made in a contract cannot be fully performed in a year *from when the contract was made*, all the promises in the contract are within the Statute of Frauds and thus must be in writing to be enforceable. This rule is not quite as broad as it sounds, for judges do not like letting contracts fall within the statute of frauds if they feel that the result would lead to injustice, so they tend to construe the requirement that a promise "cannot" be performed within a year quite strictly

iii. It is only when, by its own terms, completed performance of a promise is *impossible* within a year of its making that the statute applies
   1. If completed performance of a promise is theoretically possible, even if factually unlikely, within one year *from the date it was made*, the contract is outside the Statute and can be enforced even if oral
      a. Ex: Stoned Philips' Construction Company is awarded a contract for $2 billion to build an office tower twice as high and twice as large as the Sears Tower in Chicago. While it is factually unlikely that such a project could be completed in less than a year, there is nothing inherent in the contract itself that makes the completion of performance impossible within a year, and therefore the Statute does not apply
      b. Ex: Brian agrees to serve as Kendogg's butler for a two year period. Since by its very terms Brian's promise cannot be completed within a year, the contract is within the Statute and must be in writing to be enforceable
      c. Ex: On September 1, Pigpen agrees to work as an assistant to Mr. Flakes for a three month period beginning next July 15. The contract is within the Statute, for by its terms it **cannot be completed** within one year **of its making**. Thus, it must be in writing to be enforceable

VIII. VOIDABILITY, A FANCY NAME FOR CONTRACT DEFENSES: MISTAKE AND MISUNDERSTANDING

A. THE MISTAKE DOCTRINE
  i. A contract entered into by mistake is voidable
B. DEFINITION OF "MISTAKE"
  i. **A mistake is a belief that is not in accord with the true facts** [Rest. §151]
  ii. Mistake does **not** mean an improvident act, e.g., the making of a contract in which a party lost money
  iii. Erroneous belief as to the future is not a "mistake"
  iv. Mistake of law can be a mistake of fact
     1. A contracting party may have an erroneous belief as to the legal consequence of its promise in a contract. The existing law at the time the contract is made is generally considered a "fact," and thus, **relief can be granted for a mistaken belief as to the operation of the law**, assuming all the other elements for applying the mistake doctrine are present

v. "Mistake" distinguished from "Misunderstanding"
   1. A misunderstanding occurs when two parties attach different meanings to the same term in their agreement. As such, it is not an erroneous belief as to a fact, and it is analytically distinct from the mistake doctrine

C. UNILATERAL AND MUTUAL MISTAKE
   i. In general, **it is easier for the party adversely affected by the mistake to get relief when the mistake is mutual rather than when it is unilateral**

D. MUTUAL MISTAKE DEFINED
   i. Mutual mistake occurs when both parties to a contract are under substantially the same erroneous belief as to the true facts present in an exchange [Rest. §152]. If a party is adversely affected by a contract entered into mutual mistake, the contract is **voidable** at the option of that party

E. UNILATERAL MISTAKE DEFINED
   i. A unilateral mistake occurs when only one party to a contract has an erroneous belief as to the true facts present in an exchange [Rest. 153]
   ii. Elements necessary to establish unilateral mistake [Rest. §153]:
      1. The mistake must be as to a **basic assumption** on which the contract was made
         a. The mistake must change the essential nature of the contract
      2. The mistake must have a **material effect** on the agreed exchange of performances
         a. It must be shown that it would simply be too unfair to enforce the bargain as called for in the contract
      3. The party seeking to avoid the contract **must not bear the risk** of that mistake. Under Rest. §154, there are three alternative grounds for finding that a party bore the risk of the mistake:
         a. The risk was allocated to the party by express agreement of the parties (very rare)
         b. The party is aware, at the time the contract is made, that he has only a limited knowledge of the true facts, but decides to treat that limited knowledge as sufficient
         c. As a matter of law the court finds it reasonable to place the risk of the mistake on that party
      4. **Either** of the following:
         a. The effect of the mistake is such that enforcement against the mistaken party would be **unconscionable**
         b. The non-mistaken party either had reason to know of the mistake or caused the mistake

      iii. Example of Mistaken Bid Cases
1. Sully is a general contractor, and owner of "The Shop". Not being very astute in math, he submits a very low bid to Guido, the developer of "Swamplands Shopping Center", a new mall in Up Saddle River, New Jersey. After the contract has been awarded Sully discovers he made an arithmetic error in the bidding process, and will end up losing money on the project. To get relief Sully must show all of the above elements. Sully's difficulty will lie in showing that either enforcement of the contract will be *unconscionable* or that Guido had reason to know of the mistake or caused it. For example, if all the other bids for the project were $10-13 million, and Sully's bid was $6 million, a case could be made that Guido had reason to know of the mistake

      iv. Effect of Unilateral Mistake
1. If a party can establish the requisites for relief under a unilateral mistake theory, the contract is **voidable** by that party. That is, the mistaken party can enforce it, or may disaffirm it, at that party's option
    a. **Restitution** required upon voidance of contract entered into unilateral mistake
        i. Both parties have to give restitution to each other for any benefits conferred

F. THE "MISUNDERSTANDING" DOCTRINE
      i. **Misunderstanding occurs when the parties agree to a term in their contract, but each has a different meaning of the term** [Rest. §20]
1. Ex: If the parties agree to the purchase and sale of ten tons of steel, but one party believes it to be metric tons and the other believes it to be English tons, the issue is one of misunderstanding, not mistake

      ii. Distinguishing "misunderstanding" from "mistake"
1. Misunderstanding is a **formation issue**, i.e., the misunderstanding doctrine governs whether the parties in fact have a contract and, if so, what its terms are. The mistake doctrine, on the other hand, assumes the existence of a valid contract, and the issue is whether a party may void it due to a mistaken belief that is not in accord with the true facts

      iii. Effect of Misunderstanding
1. **If neither party knows, or has reason to know, of the meaning of a material term attached by the other, then no contract is formed** [Rest. §20(1)]
2. However, if the parties have different meanings of a material term, but one party knows of the misunderstanding

and the other party does not, **a contract is formed** and the meaning of the disputed term is the one believed by the party who did not know of the misunderstanding [Rest. §20(2)]
3. Note that misunderstanding must be as to a **material term** for the misunderstanding doctrine to apply, and if established, entitles the party to rescission
    a. Ex: ***Raffles v. Wichelhaus***. Buyer and seller agreed upon the sale of cotton to be sent on the ship *The Peerless* from Bombay. Unfortunately, there were two ships named *The Peerless*, and they each left Bombay a few months apart. The 1st *Peerless* left in October, the 2nd *Peerless* in December. The buyer believed the contract called for shipment on the 1st *Peerless*; the seller believed it called for shipment on the 2nd *Peerless*. **Held:** As neither party knew (or had reason to know) of the meaning attached to the term "*The Peerless*" by the other, no contract was ever formed since there was **no manifestation of mutual assent**, as is necessary for contract formation. Thus, while the seller was not in breach for sending the goods on the 2nd *Peerless*, the buyer was also not in breach for refusing to accept them when they arrived later than expected for no contract was ever formed between them
    b. Ex: The facts are the same as in ***Raffles***, except assume both buyer and seller knew there were two ships named *The Peerless*, and the buyer knew the seller meant the 2nd *Peerless*, but the seller knew the buyer meant the 1st *Peerless*. In that case, once again no contract would be formed, regardless of which ship the goods were eventually shipped on, for each party was aware of the other's misunderstanding, and chose to go ahead anyway without correcting it
    c. Ex: The facts are the same as in ***Raffles***, except assume the seller (who is in Bombay) knows there are two ships called *The Peerless*. Seller intends to ship on the later departing ship, but is confident that buyer expects the goods to be shipped on the 1st *Peerless*. In that case a contract **is** formed, and it is for shipment on the 1st *Peerless* under the rule of Rest. §20(2)

G. ***** <u>**EXAM APPROACH TO MISTAKE AND MISUNDERSTANDING ISSUES**</u> *****
    i. Make sure that you ascertain whether either party was laboring under a mistake as to an existing **fact** *at the time of the making* of the contract, for purposes of mistake; or laboring under a different meaning of a contractual term, for purposes of misunderstanding
    ii. If so, then set forth the elements that determine whether each of the doctrines will apply in the case. Find the facts in the problem that correspond to each element of the doctrine, and then argue those facts, making sure to reach a definite conclusion

IX. VOIDABILITY, A FANCY NAME FOR CONTRACT DEFENSES: UNCONSCIONABILITY

A. THE UNCONSCIONABILITY DOCTRINE
    i. A contract is unconscionable if it sets forth a deal "no man in his senses" would make on the one hand, and no honest or fair man would accept on the other = moral aspect
    ii. A court is directed to step in and correct a situation in which one party makes too good a deal for himself, **even in the absence of duress, undue influence, misrepresentation, etc.**

B. UNCONSCIONABILITY APPLIES TO UCC AND NON-UCC TRANSACTIONS
    i. The modern unconscionability doctrine emanates from §2-302 of the UCC. However, it has been routinely applied to non-UCC transactions, and is now included in the Restatement at §208

C. EFFECT OF UNCONSCIONABILITY UNDER MODERN CONTRACT LAW
    i. The decision as to whether a contract, or any part of it, is unconscionable is a decision for the court and not the jury [UCC §2-302, Rest. §208]
    ii. Once a court determines unconscionability is present, it is empowered:
        1. **To refuse enforcement of the entire contract**
        2. **To enforce the remainder of the contract without the unconscionable clause or clauses**
        3. **To modify or limit application of any clause to avoid an unjust result**

D. ELEMENTS NECESSARY TO ESTABLISH UNCONSCIONABILITY
    i. **All clauses or contracts found to be unconscionable have some combination of**
        1. *Procedural* unconscionability, AND
        2. *Substantive* unconscionability
    ii. Definition of "procedural" unconscionability
        1. **Absence of meaningful choice**, made up of:
            a. **Oppression**, i.e., unequal bargaining power, AND

i. Monopoly – market or situational (ex: hooked in by a frequent flyer program)
            b. **Surprise**, i.e, the fact that the unconscionable clause is typically hidden in the numerous terms and legal jargon of a written statement and is not really a bargained for, or dickered, term
        iii. Definition of "substantive" unconscionability
            1. **Terms that are unreasonably favorable to one party**
        iv. Some combination of **both** procedural and substantive unconscionability is necessary for application of the doctrine
            1. The greater the presence of one type of unconscionability, the less the presence of the other is necessary before the doctrine applies
        v. Unconscionability applies to conditions present at the time of making the contract
            1. The procedural and substantive aspects of unconscionability are examined at the time the contract was made, not at the time of its performance
        vi. Note on Adhesion Contracts
            1. It is sometimes said that all adhesion contracts, i.e., contracts where one party dictates non-negotiable terms and the other party must agree to "adhere" to them or not enter a bargain, are unconscionable. This is not true. While the existence of an adhesion contract is evidence of a lack of bargaining power on one side, it is not conclusive evidence either that the terms were unfair or that the "weaker" party did not know, appreciate, and freely agree to be bound by those terms
    E. UNCONSCIONABILITY NOT LIMITED TO CONSUMER TRANSACTIONS. See *A&M Produce v. FMC Corp.*
    F. UNCONSCIONABILITY APPLIED TO CLAUSES WHICH LIMIT REMEDIES OR DISCLAIM WARRANTIES
        i. In §§2-719 and 2-316 respectively, the UCC explicitly provides that a party's remedies upon breach can be limited, and that a buyer's warranties can be disclaimed
        ii. While such clauses are specifically permitted by the Code, they are only enforceable if they are not unreasonably unfair under the circumstances, and if the other party is not the victim of oppression and/or surprise
    G. The major example of unconscionability: *Williams v. Walker-Thomas Furniture Co.*
        i. The court held that cross-collateralization clauses were specifically permitted by the UCC, but their inclusion in the contract at issue was nevertheless found to be unconscionable:
            1. Procedural unconscionability (absence of meaningful choice)

                a. Oppression: unequal bargaining power because Ms. Williams' credit history did not allow her to buy her furniture in any other way than through credit with cross-collateralization clauses. That is, Ms. Williams could not have bargained for a contract without the cross-collateralization clause, she **had no choice**
                b. Surprise: The cross-collateralization clause was not pointed out or explained to her, and was hidden in the contract
            2. Substantive unconscionability
                a. The store was not seeking just to repossess the last goods purchased, but all the goods she had bought there since 1958, many of which had been fully paid for
    H. **EXAM APPROACH TO UNCONSCIONABILITY ISSUES**
        i. When confronted with a contract that is extremely favorable for one party, first check for evidence of incapacity, duress, undue influence, or misrepresentation. If there are no facts to support any of those theories, *then* check to see if:
            1. There is an absence of meaningful choice on the part of the aggrieved party, AND
            2. The terms of the contract are sufficiently unfair to the aggrieved party

X. **THE PAROL EVIDENCE RULE: SUBSTANTIVE DOCTRINE**

   A. THE PAROL EVIDENCE RULE GENERALLY
        i. The Parol Evidence Rule (PER) regulates when a party to a written contract may introduce evidence that the parties had reached an agreement as to a particular term when that term, for some reason, did not appear in the final version of the written contract
        ii. **At the heart of this rule is a common sense preference held by contract law for only enforcing the final agreement of the contracting parties. When they cannot agree as to what their final agreement was, the parol evidence rule provides a way for a court to determine what terms the court will enforce**
        iii. Parol evidence can be written or oral
            1. The previous agreement that is not included in the writings is usually oral, but it does not have to be so. If a party has a draft written contract and wants to show that a particular term in the draft, but not in the final version, of the written agreement was really part of the final deal, that written draft is analyzed the same way as if the alleged parol agreement was oral

B. STATEMENT OF THE PAROL EVIDENCE RULE
   i. The parol evidence rule operates whenever there is a writing evidencing an agreement, where one party seeks to introduce evidence that the parties had agreed to other terms before contracting that are not found in the written contract. The rule governing whether that party will be allowed to introduce evidence of those allegedly agreed upon, but excluded (from the final writing) terms, i.e., evidence of "parol" agreements, is in two parts:
      1. **If the writing is partially integrated:**
         a. **no evidence of a term agreed prior to, or contemporaneous with, the writing, whether written or oral, can be introduced *if* such term will *contradict* a term of the writing, but it *can* be admitted to supplement or explain the writing**, AND
      2. **If the writing is totally integrated:**
         a. **no evidence of prior or contemporaneous agreements, whether written or oral, can be admitted** [Rest. §§ 210, 213, 215, and 216]
   ii. Partially Integrated Agreements
      1. A writing is "integrated" if it contains at least one term intended by the parties to be their final expression of agreement as to that term [Rest. §209]
      2. A writing is "partially integrated" if the parties intended it to be the final expression of at least one of the terms it contains, but do not intend it to be a final expression of *all* terms of their agreement. That is, the writing contains some, but not all, of the final terms of their agreement [Rest. §210(2)]. If a writing is found to be partially integrated, under the parol evidence rule a party may introduce evidence of other terms previously agreed to, but not now found in the writing, so long as they do not "contradict" any term found in the writing
   iii. Totally Integrated Agreements
      1. A writing is totally integrated if it is intended to be the complete and exclusive expression of *all* the terms of the deal [Rest. §210(1)]
      2. If a writing is found to be totally integrated, no evidence of **any** term not found in the writings is allowed
      3. However, one can introduce other terms to *explain* terms found in the writing [Rest. §214(c)]
   iv. How to determine whether an agreement is integrated at all, partially integrated, or totally integrated
      1. Essentially the issue is this: should contract law allow a party freely to put on evidence of the alleged prior agreements, and see whether the jury believes or

disbelieves the party's testimony; or should contract law be restrictive in allowing a party's ability to introduce such evidence, thereby expressing a preference for enforcing only the terms of a signed, written contract? Contract law's approach to this problem has changed over time

2. Williston View: Look only to "Four Corners" of the writing to determine integration
    a. Court judges the completeness of the agreement based not only on the writings, but also on the "surrounding circumstances", e.g., the time frame under which it was made, how it was negotiated, by whom it was negotiated, etc.
    b. However, **proffered testimony by the parties of what was allegedly agreed to during the negotiations will not be permitted**
3. Corbin and Restatement View: All Evidence Surrounding the Making of the Contract Should be Examined by the Court to Determine Integration [Rest. §§210, 214]
    a. A party can introduce all relevant evidence (at least to the judge) to show the circumstances surrounding the making of the writing in order to show the writing is not completely integrated or even that it is not integrated at all
    b. The thought is that letting a judge hear the evidence out of the presence of the jury will not harm the fact finding process
    c. If after hearing the testimony a judge decides that there is enough evidence so that a jury *could* find that the written document is not the complete and final agreement of the parties, it will be deemed partially integrated and evidence of *non-contradictory* parol terms can be admitted
4. Determination of integration is to be made by court, not jury, and the effects of such determination
    a. Under all views, the determination as to whether the writing is integrated at all, partially integrated, or totally integrated is to be made by the court outside the presence of the jury [Rest. §210(3)]. If the writing is determined to be partially integrated, evidence of non-contradictory terms is admissible and can be presented to the jury. If the writing is determined to be totally integrated, no evidence of other terms will be admitted
        i. Effect of "Merger/Integration" Clauses
            1. A merger clause is usually found at the end of a written agreement and

will say something like "The parties to this contract hereby affirm that this writing expresses the final and complete terms of their agreement. All prior agreements are *merged* into this contract"
2. The obvious intent of such clauses is to ensure that a court will find the document totally integrated
3. The general rule is that such clauses have persuasive, but not determinative, effect on the question of whether the parties intended the agreement to be totally integrated

v. Determination of whether a term is "contradictory" and thus cannot be introduced even with a partially integrated writing: the Restatement's "might naturally" test
1. [Rest. §216] A parol term does not "contradict" a term in the writing so long as it is a "consistent additional term"
2. **A term is a consistent additional term if, under the circumstances, it is one that "*might naturally* have been omitted from the writing."** That is, the test is whether, if the parties had really agreed to such a term, it is the kind of term that might naturally have been left out when they finally reduced their agreement to writing [Rest. §216(2)(b)]
3. However, if it is a term that, had the parties agreed to it, probably **would have been included** in the writings, i.e., it is a kind of term that naturally would **not** be left out of a final writing, then it is a contradictory term and cannot be introduced
   a. Ex: ***Mitchill v. Lath.*** Purchaser of land attempted to show that, as a part of the purchase price, seller had orally agreed to remove an ice house from an adjacent piece of property that seller also controlled. The ice house interfered with the view from the piece of property buyer had purchased. The written contract of sale, however, made no mention of the removal of the ice house. **Held**: If the seller had really agreed to remove the ice house, it was the type of term which probably would have been included somewhere in the documents exchanged by the parties. As such, it was *not* the kind of term that "might naturally" be omitted from the writings. Hence, it was a "contradictory" term, and evidence of its having been agreed to could not be presented

to the trier of fact, even if the contract was partially integrated
- b. Ex: Kumar was interested in selling some property he owned for $7,500. Kumar was also about to undergo some plastic surgery and asked his doctor Lou if he would be interested in purchasing it. Incidentally, Lou after graduating from U. Penn Wharton and working as an investment banker at Goldnut Sacks for a few years, abruptly quit and went to medical school because, in his words he "didn't want to be a whore lusting after money like bankers and lawyers." Anyways, Lou said he would purchase the property from Kumar, and as Lou's fee for the surgery was $7,500, they agreed to a barter exchange. However, for tax reasons, the conveyance documents recited that the price for the land was "$7,500" and said nothing about the barter agreement. Kumar now sues for $7,500 in cash. Lou will be able to introduce evidence of the agreed barter payment term, for it is the kind of term that, under the circumstances, might naturally be omitted from the written embodiment of the agreement

C. SITUATIONS IN WHICH THE PAROL EVIDENCE RULE DOES NOT APPLY
  i. In the situations discussed below, the parol evidence rule does not in any way limit the introduction of evidence concerning any terms previously agreed to by the parties regardless of whether the final contract is totally integrated, and regardless of whether they contradict the writing
  ii. Agreements made after the contract has been formed
    1. Such agreements, whether oral or written, are **modifications** to an existing contract and are governed by the rules on modifications
  iii. Where a party introduces evidence to show there was no valid agreement
    1. If the evidence is intended to show the writing was a joke, forgery, etc. it is freely admissible
  iv. Evidence of a condition precedent
    1. The parol evidence rule will also not exclude evidence that the contract was subject to a parol condition precedent. The reason is that if such a condition was agreed to, and if it has not been fulfilled, no duty set forth in the written agreement would be enforceable
  v. Evidence of a failure to pay consideration
    1. If a party wants to introduce proof that the purported consideration evidenced in the writing was never

exchanged, the parol evidence rule will not keep such evidence from being presented
- a. PER does apply to Option Contracts
  - i. Because option contracts can be enforced on the basis of purported, but unperformed consideration, this exception to the PER does not apply to them
- vi. Evidence of facts establishing that the contract is voidable
  1. A party who wants to introduce evidence that would entitle him to void the contract on the grounds of misrepresentation, duress, undue influence, illegality, mistake, or *unconscionability* will not be precluded from doing so by the PER
- vii. **Evidence as to a meaning of a term found in the written contract**
  1. In this case, the issue is one of interpretation, not of the PER

D. CONTEMPORANEOUS "SIDE" AGREEMENTS
  - i. Parties with standardized contracts are sometimes reluctant to delete or amend them, even if the parties actually agree to a deal on terms different from those found in the standard agreement
  - ii. In such cases they will often enter into "side letter agreements" which specifically recite that contemporaneous with the signing of the standardized agreement the parties intended to change a provision of that agreement
  - iii. The effect of such side letter agreements is that the "writing" to which the PER applies consists of **both the standard form and the side letter agreement**, and the terms found in both such writings become the written contract

E. PAROL TERMS, EVEN WHEN ADMITTED, DO NOT AUTOMATICALLY BECOME PART OF THE CONTRACT
  - i. All that happens when a judge allows the admission of parol evidence is that the party proffering the evidence has a **chance to convince** the trier of fact that the previous agreement existed
  - ii. If the trier of fact does not believe the party seeking to prove the agreement, the parol term does **not** become part of the contract
  - iii. If, but only if, the trier of fact believes the evidence, then those terms become part of the agreement, and any claim of breach is viewed in light of the final written contract plus the parol terms

F. ***** <u>**EXAM APPROACH TO PAROL EVIDENCE ISSUES**</u> *****
  - i. Determine whether the written contract itself is partially or completely integrated, remembering that the "Corbin" view is the majority view today
  - ii. If it is totally integrated, no parol evidence can be introduced
  - iii. If it is partially integrated, then parol evidence is admissible to explain and supplement the written contract, but not to contradict

it, recalling that it is the "might naturally" test that determines whether the parol language contradicts or supplements the written contract

iv. If you are unable to introduce parol evidence, whether because the written contract is totally integrated, because the parol evidence is contradictory rather than supplementary, check to see if one of the "exceptions" to the parol evidence rule applies that will allow admission of the evidence anyway

v. If you are able to introduce the parol evidence, the term does not automatically become part of the contract. That is up to the trier of fact

XI. THE PAROL EVIDENCE RULE: UCC §2-202

A. UCC §2-202: AN ATTEMPT TO COMBINE THE PAROL EVIDENCE RULE WITH INTERPRETATION RULES
  i. The provision attempts to regulate both:
    1. What terms are included in the contract (PER)
    2. When extrinsic evidence is admissible to show the parties' particular meaning of a term (interpretation)
B. HOW TO APPROACH A §2-202 PROBLEM
  i. As with all UCC problems, the first step is to ensure that the transaction is one to which Article 2 of the UCC applies
    1. UCC §2-105: UCC applies to sales of goods (movable objects); therefore, real property and service contracts are not covered
  ii. Ascertain whether the writing is partially integrated, totally integrated, or not integrated at all. The rules governing this determination are the same as those for non-UCC transactions
  iii. Once that determination is made, the following rules govern when parol evidence may be introduced and what extrinsic evidence is admissible to explain the terms found in the agreement:
    1. When the writing is partially integrated
      a. If the writing is partially integrated, then no evidence of any supplementary term that **contradicts** any term in the writing will be admitted under §2-202
        i. Evidence of "Contradictory" terms cannot be used to *supplement* the contract
          1. This is the same as in the C/L PER
        ii. "Contradictory" terms are judged under the **"Would Certainly"** test
          1. [UCC §2-202, Com 3] Under the "would certainly" test, the question is **whether the proffered term is the type that *would certainly* have**

been included in the final agreement of the parties had it, in fact, been agreed to
2. There does not seem to be much of a difference between this test and the C/L "might naturally" test. Perhaps here there is a required mental state of *gross negligence*?
b. Evidence of course of performance, course of dealing, and usage of trade can be introduced to *explain* a term *found in the contract*
2. When the writing is totally integrated
a. As under the C/L PER, if the writing as governed by Article 2 is totally integrated, no evidence of any supplementary terms is allowed
b. However, one can introduce other terms to *explain* terms found in the writing
C. SITUATIONS WHERE UCC §2-202 DOES NOT APPLY
   i. The situations are the same as those for the C/L PER
D. ***** **EXAM APPROACH TO §2-202 ISSUES** *****
   i. The exam approach is the same as for the C/L PER with one exception:
   ii. The only major change is that the test for whether the parol term supplements or contradicts the written contract is the "would certainly" test under §2-202, rather than the "might naturally" test of common law

XII. PERFORMANCE AND BREACH OF DUTIES: IN GENERAL

A. PERFORMANCE AND BREACH
   i. **Breach** is a strict liability concept
B. THE ROLE OF CONSTRUCTIVE CONDITIONS
   i. Constructive conditions are conditions implied by a court as a matter of law to help a court ascertain the rights and duties of the parties. The three main functions of constructive conditions are:
      1. To help determine the order of performance
      2. To help determine which party, if either, is in breach
      3. If there is a breach, to help determine whether it is material or immaterial
   ii. While there are numerous constructive conditions in the case law, Most Prof 's will usually only talk/care about three: (1) tender (2) the requirement that a party whose performance takes time must completely perform before he is entitled to payment and (3) the absence of material breach

C. TENDER
   i. "Tender" is fulfilled by a party's **offer of performance** coupled with a manifest **present ability** to perform [Rest. §238]
   ii. **One party must tender performance before the duties of the other can be enforced**
      1. Ex: 1L J.V.D and 1L B.R. are in a contract whereby B.R. has promised to deliver his watch to J.V.D at Thursday's bar review, in return for J.V.D's promise to pay $125 for the watch at the same time. On Thursday night, in a drunken stupor J.V.D shows B.R., who himself is very inebriated, that he has the money and tells him he will hand him the money once he tenders the watch. B.R. refuses to show him the watch until he actually hands him the money. They leave stumbling out of the bar, cursing at each other, almost ready to engage in fisticuffs. **Held: (K.Dogg, J.)** J.V.D. is entitled to sue B.R. for breach, because by tendering his performance, he made B.R.'s duty to deliver the watch enforceable.

D. ORDER OF PERFORMANCE
   i. If the performance of each party can be accomplished simultaneously, then each party is under an obligation to perform concurrently
   ii. If the performance of one party will take time, and performance of the other will not, performance by the party whose performance will take time is a constructive condition of the performance of the party whose performance will not take time
   iii. Note that these rules are presumptive only and can be changed by the parties themselves in their contract

E. MATERIAL AND IMMATERIAL (OR PARTIAL) BREACH
   i. A material breach occurs when a party fails to perform a duty due under a contract which results in the unexcused non-occurrence of a constructive condition of exchange
   ii. An immaterial breach is a failure of a party to perform a duty due under a contract that results in the *excused* non-occurrence of a constructive condition of exchange
   iii. Total breach is **not** synonymous with material breach. A total breach is what a material breach becomes if, after a reasonable period of time, the material breach is neither cured nor waived
   iv. Minor, partial, and immaterial breach **are** synonyms
   v. Consequences of deciding that a breach is material or immaterial
      1. Upon a material breach, the non-breaching party is entitled immediately to *suspend* his duties under the contract without contractual liability
      2. However, upon an *immaterial* breach, the non-breaching party *must* **continue to perform** or itself be in breach

                a. The non-breaching party still has the right to sue for **damages** resulting from the breach. It is just that when the breach is *material*, **in addition to the right to collect damages**, the non-breaching party is **also entitled to suspend performance**
        vi. The only situation in which the materiality of the breach matters: bilateral contracts in which there are executory duties remaining on both sides at the time of the breach
            1. There are many times in which it is irrelevant whether a breach is material or immaterial, in these cases, a breach is just a breach
            2. The only time it matters whether it is material or not is when the parties have entered into a bilateral contract, and there are unperformed duties remaining on **both** sides at the time of the breach
            3. This is because it is only in such a situation that whether the non-breaching party still has to perform is an issue
        vii. **How to determine whether a breach is material or immaterial**
            1. In deciding whether a particular breach results in an unexcused failure of a constructive condition (thus, a material breach), Rest. §241 states that the following factors need to be weighed:
                a. The extent to which the non-breaching party will be deprived of the reasonably expected benefit of his bargain
                b. The extent to which the non-breaching party can be fully compensated for the breach if made to stay in the contract and complete performance
                c. The extent to which the breaching party will suffer a forfeiture if the breach is declared material and the non-breaching party need not perform under the contract
                d. The likelihood the breaching party will cure his or her failure
                e. The good or bad faith exhibited by the breaching party in breaching the contract
            2. The test for when a material breach becomes a *total breach*: when the breach is neither cured nor excused after a reasonable time
                a. The non-breaching party **may terminate** his duties under the contract only when the material breach ripens into a **total breach**
                b. This occurs at the end of a reasonable period of time if the breach has been neither cured nor excused
                    i. If the material breach is cured or waived within a reasonable time period, the

formerly material breach is transformed into an immaterial one, and the non-breaching party must continue performance. Of course, the non-breaching party **may sue** for damages resulting from the breaching party's immaterial breach
3. The Substantial Performance Doctrine: Classic Application of the Immaterial Breach Doctrine
    a. So long as a party has "substantially performed" a duty under a contract, any discrepancy between the actual performance and the promised performance will be deemed an *immaterial* breach
    b. In theory, the substantial performance doctrine could be applied to every breach of a bilateral contract with unperformed duties remaining on both sides. However, in practice it is generally applied only to breaches of contracts involving services, esp. those dealing with construction contracts [Rest. §237, Com. d]
    c. **How to determine whether a promise has been substantially performed.** Factors to consider:
        i. How much of the reasonably expected benefit under the contract has the non-breaching party received under the contract at the time of the breach
        ii. How great a forfeiture will the breaching party suffer if the breach is deemed material
        iii. How completely will damages alone compensate the non-breaching party. Sometimes damages are not sufficient if there are strong idiosyncratic preferences on the part of the non-breaching party
        iv. The good or bad faith of the breaching party
        v. How likely is it that rectifying the breach will result in "economic waste" rather than actually providing a benefit for the non-breaching party
4. In every generation, there is a case that is a landmark case, one in which the course of American jurisprudence is forever changed. The following case is not one of them. Even though most Prof's spend a lot of time on it. Yes, it is……***JACOB & YOUNGS v. KENT***
    a. Kent's argument was that if Jacob & Youngs did not fully perform the Reading pipe promise, the contractor would be in *material* breach, thereby suspending and ultimately discharging Kent's duty

     to make the remaining progress payments due under the contract
- b. **Held**: The inadvertent use of the wrong pipe by Jacob & Youngs only amounted to an immaterial breach under the *substantial performance* doctrine. Nevertheless, because there was deviation from full and complete performance by Jacob & Youngs, there was a breach and Kent could sue for any damage he might have suffered as a result of the wrong pipe being installed (which likely would be nothing)
- c. **Reasoning**
    - i. Kent had received substantially all the benefit he could reasonably expect under the contract, i.e., he got a completed house for the price stated, with an equivalent quality of pipe throughout
    - ii. To have the breach declared material would result in an unfair forfeiture to Jacob & Youngs, i.e., to deny the company relief under the contract on an inadvertent mistake that resulted in no objective detriment to Kent would be unjust
    - iii. Damages could compensate Kent for any harm he might have suffered due to the breach
    - iv. The breach was inadvertent, and thus was a "good faith" breach
    - v. Having the breach declared material would result in economic waste, i.e., it would cost Jacob & Youngs a huge amount of money to rip out the walls and re-lay the pipe, with no corresponding benefit to Kent for doing so. Thus, any money spent remedying the breach (as opposed to paying for damages resulting from the breach) would be an economic waste

F. ******* <u>EXAM APPROACH TO BREACH ISSUES</u> *******
1. Make sure that a breach has occurred, i.e., that a party's failure to perform completely what has been promised under a contract is not subject to a defense or some other doctrine whereby the failure to perform is justified or excused, including checking to make sure performance by the other party was tendered

2. If a breach has occurred, then check to see whether the contract was a bilateral one with unexecuted duties at the time of the breach
    a. If it was, determine whether the breach was material or immaterial, realizing that in a material breach, the aggrieved party may suspend performance, and keeping in mind the "first" material breach doctrine
        i. If the breach was material, check to see if it was total, realizing that when a material breach ripens into a total breach, the aggrieved party's performance is discharged and the contract is over
    b. If the contract was not a bilateral contract with unexecuted duties by both sides at the time of the breach, then go to step 3
3. Make sure you write on your exam that the non-breaching party is entitled to damages regardless of whether the breach is material or immaterial, and then analyze the damages recoverable by the aggrieved party

XIII. REMEDIES: EQUITABLE REMEDIES (SPECIFIC PERFORMANCE)

A. EQUITABLE RELIEF GENERALLY
   i. The four most common types of equitable relief granted for breach of contract claims by American courts are:
      1. **Specific Performance**, where a court orders a party actually to perform the very duty that he promised to perform in the contract [Rest. §360, Com. b]
      2. **Prohibitory Injunctions**, where a court orders a party to refrain from doing something that would interfere with his ability to carry out the performance promised under the contract
      3. **Unilateral Rescission**, where a court orders the contract terminated and the parties to return all benefits received under the contract up until that point
         a. If one party does not freely enter into a contract due to misrepresentation or mistake, and wants to get out of the deal all together
         b. Each party must make *restitution* to the other
      4. **Reformation**, where a court orders a contract re-written to reflect the parties' true intentions
B. REQUIREMENTS FOR OBTAINING EQUITABLE RELIEF FOR BREACH OF CONTRACT
   i. Money damages are the normal remedy for contractual breach, and only in the extraordinary case will equitable relief be granted

ii. To obtain an order for equitable relief, the non-breaching party must establish:
   1. That an award for **money damages** is "**inadequate**" to put the non-breaching party in the position the party would have been had the contract been performed [Rest. §359]. The court considers the following factors (or to put it another way, all three of these factors have to be satisfied in order to get money damages):
      a. The difficulty in proving damages with reasonable certainty [Rest. §360(1)]
         i. Ex: Larry decides to open a hot dog stand in a posh mall on Long Island. The mall breaches his lease and rents the space to someone else just before he is about to move in. It takes Larry six months before he can find premises, and he ends up opening his stand in a strip mall in Newark. Larry will pay the same rent for the replacement premises, and therefore suffers no *direct damages*; however Larry could argue that the Long Island location has many intangible benefits that money cannot purchase such as more affluent customers and a nicer ambience
      b. The difficulty in procuring a suitable substitute performance upon an award of monetary damages [Rest. §360(2)]
         i. **Land is always considered unique**
      c. The likelihood that award of damages could not be collected [Rest. §360(3)]
   2. That there are **no undue "practical limitations"** on a court's ability to grant equitable relief [Rest. §§362, 366, and 367]
      a. There are administrative burdens involved in supervising a party's compliance with a court order. When those burdens get too great, a court will not order specific performance or an injunction, even if a damage award would not reliably put the innocent party in the position he would have been had the contract been performed
      b. A typical list of the practical problems of enforcement that courts consider in deciding whether to order equitable relief includes
         i. Whether the terms of the contract are sufficiently certain so as to provide a basis for an appropriate court order [Rest. §362]

ii. Whether the nature and the magnitude of the performance promised in the contract would impose a supervisory burden on the court that is disproportionate to the advantages to be gained from specific enforcement and to the harm to be suffered from its denial [Rest. §366]
iii. Whether the contract calls for personal services [Rest. §367(1)]
1. Cannot force a "unique" person to complete the contract. Can get an **injunction** prohibiting him for working for someone else during the contract period
3. That an award of equitable relief will **not itself be unfair** by violating one of the "equitable principles" governing the grant of equitable relief [Rest. §§364, 365]. The court considers the following equitable principles in deciding whether to issue an order for specific performance or an injunction:
    a. Whether the act or forbearance compelled by the grant of equitable relief would be **contrary to public policy** [Rest. §365]
    b. Whether specific enforcement of the contract would be unjust because the breaching party's assent to the contract was **induced by an unfair business practice** [Rest. §364(1)(a)]
        i. The practices of the non breaching party during the negotiation of the contract are deemed "sharp" or unfair, though not outright fraudulent
        ii. The breaching party may still be liable in money damages arising from his non-performance
    c. Whether specific enforcement of the contract would **cause unreasonable hardship** to the breaching party. Money damages may be ordered instead [Rest. §364(1)(b)]
        i. Ex: ***Peevyhouse v. Garland Coal & Mining Co.*** Donnie Brasco owns property in a desolate part of the state that lies fallow. Mining Co. acquires from Donnie the right to strip mine for copper on the land, promising in its contract that it will refill the hole after it is done mining and will restore the land so that it will be indistinguishable

54

from the surrounding countryside. After finishing mining, Mining Co. discovers it will cost over $4,000,000 to fill the hole and otherwise perform its promise. The decreased fair market value of the land as a result of having a hole in it is only $30,000. Mining Co. does not fill the hole. Donnie is probably not entitled to an order of specific performance given the disproportionate economic hardship such an order would cause to Mining Co.
1. This may be justified on the grounds of economic waste
2. Plaintiffs such as Donnie may really not want Mining Co. to specifically perform. They simply **want a court to issue an order requiring the promisor to perform**, which they will later agree not to enforce upon a payment of an amount less than the cost of performance (See *Jacob & Youngs v. Kent*). Accordingly, a plaintiff such as Donnie is coming into court with "unclean hands" and should be denied equitable relief for that reason as well
d. Whether the court is satisfied that specific enforcement of the contract **would not result in the non-performance** of a substantial part of the agreed exchange by the non-breaching party [Rest. §363]
i. No order of specific performance will be issued unless a substantial part of the return performance due to the breaching party **has already been rendered**, or unless the court determines to its satisfaction that such **return performance is likely** [Rest. §363]

C. ****** EXAM APPROACH TO EQUITABLE RELIEF ISSUES ******
   i. It is very unlikely that an entire one hour exam problem will turn on equitable relief issues. Rather, whether a party is entitled to equitable, as opposed to legal, relief will much more likely be one of several issues in a problem dealing with breach and remedies
   ii. As a consequence, when you are in a problem that tests remedies, you should make sure:
   1. Damages will fail to put the breaching party in the position he would have been in had the contract been performed

2. There are no undue practical limitations in granting equitable relief
3. No "equitable principles" will be violated by an equitable award
4. If all of those elements are satisfied, then choose the most appropriate remedy: specific performance, injunction, rescission, or reformation

XIV. REMEDIES: MONEY DAMAGES

A. THE "INTEREST" ANALYSIS OF CONTRACT LAW AND THE CONCEPT OF ECONOMIC BREACH
   i. When a party enters into an enforceable contract, he does not receive a protected right to performance by the other party. Instead, he is given only a protected economic "interest" in the other party's performance
   ii. Hence, when a contract is breached the law awards damages based on the extent of interference with the non-breaching party's protected economic "interest"
   iii. The "Efficient Breach" doctrine
       1. Traditional contract law actually **encourages** breach in some situations and dictates that a party should **not** render performance. The efficient breach doctrine provides that so long as a breaching party is willing to pay for any damages caused by the breach, he **should** breach if the end result, after the breacher pays contract damages, is that the breacher will be economically better off
B. DEFINING, IDENTIFYING, AND VALUING THE ECONOMIC INTERESTS RESULTING FROM CONTRACT FORMATION
   i. The amount of the non-breaching party's recovery may well depend on which valuation method is used to ascertain the protected economic interest
   ii. **The rule is that that *non-breaching* party is entitled to pick whichever valuation method he wishes, so long as the value of the interest can be adequately proven** [Rest. §344]
   iii. Each party receives contract law's protection for three different types of economic interests. The three interests protected by contract law are **expectation, reliance, and restitution**
   iv. Types of damages recoverable by the non-breaching party
       1. **In every contract**, a party has an expectation, reliance, and a restitutionary interest
       2. The non-breaching party may seek recovery under any of the theories in every breach of contract case, and should proceed under the theory that provides a maximum reward
C. A GLOSSARY OF DAMAGES TERMINOLOGY
   i. Consequential Damages (cf. ***Hadley v. Baxendale***)

1. Consequential damages are damages which a reasonable person, present at the time of contract formation, would **not** foresee occurring as a natural result of the breach
2. Therefore, the injured party must not only prove that the loss occurred and its amount, but **also** that there was some reason the party in breach *should have known* that such a loss would follow from a breach of their particular contract
3. The injured party will only be able to recover his "consequential" damages if he can prove that something happened to put the breaching party *on notice* at the time of contract formation that the injured party would suffer an otherwise unforeseeable kind of damage upon a breach, and that the breaching party would be responsible for this reasonably unforeseeable kind of damage

ii. Direct Damages (cf. ***Hadley v. Baxendale***)
1. Direct damages are damages that may fairly and reasonably be considered as *arising naturally* from a breach of contract, as viewed by a reasonable person at the time of contract formation
2. Thus, they are the kind of damages the injured party may recover without having to make the special showing of foreseeability necessary to recover consequential damages

iii. Incidental Damages [Rest. §347(b)]
1. Incidental damages are costs incurred by the **non-breaching** party, **after** the breach, in an attempt to avoid increased loss to the breaching party
2. Often these damages are out-of-pocket costs, but they also include things like reasonable charges for storage, receipt, or transportation of improperly tendered goods, interest costs, etc.
3. So long as the decision of the non-breaching party to incur a cost in an attempt to avoid further damages to the breacher was reasonable, and so long as the amount of the expenditure was reasonable, the loss is recoverable

iv. Liquidated Damages
1. Liquidated damages are damages, the amounts of which are fixed by the parties in advance as to the amount due upon a breach of their contract. That is, as part of their contract, the parties stipulate how much one will have to pay the other upon a breach of the contract
2. Contract law does not look with favor on liquidated damages. They are only recoverable if
   a. The amount of actual damages resulting from a breach is hard to calculate with precision, AND

            b. Where the amount of the liquidated damage is a reasonable estimate of what the actual damages would be [Rest. §356]
        v. Nominal Damages
            1. A nominal damage is a small sum that has nothing to do with the actual amount of damage suffered
            2. The reason contract law provides an award for nominal damages for breach of contract is that a breach is considered a serious enough act that it should not go unpunished, even if the non-breaching party is otherwise not injured, or cannot sufficiently prove the extent of his or her injuries
    D. EXPECTATION DAMAGES: THE GENERAL MEASURE OF CONTRACT DAMAGES
        i. The economic value of a party's expectation interest is the dollar amount that would place the non-breaching party in as good a position as he would have been in **had the contract been performed** [Rest. §347, Com. a.; UCC §1-106]
        ii. Expectation recovery is **limited** by three important doctrines: certainty, foreseeability, and avoidability
        iii. Expectation damages and "Losing" contracts
            1. A party to a losing contract will typically seek a restitutionary recovery, or perhaps, a reliance damages recovery
        iv. Calculating expectation damages [Rest. §347]. Five factors that need to be accounted for in calculating expectation damages:
            1. Lost Value
                a. When a party performs a contractual promise, that performance renders value to the other party. When there is a breach, some or all of that value is not received, and is thus "lost"
                b. Calculate a dollar amount for the economic value that full performance by the breaching party would have rendered, and subtract from that figure the amount of value actually received by the non-breaching party up to the time of the breach
            2. Incidental Loss
            3. Consequential Loss
            4. Cost Avoided
                a. Recall that one consequence of another party's material breach is that the non-breaching party need not continue performance
                b. Hence, if an injured party ceases his own performance due to the other party's material breach, the injured party saves whatever monies it would have taken him to finish performance

                c. That is, if as a result of the breach certain monies are not spent by the innocent party, the breaching party must get "credit" for those costs avoided, or else he will be made to pay a sum greater than necessary to put the non-breaching party in the position he would have been in had the contract been performed
            5. Loss Avoided
                a. If materials or resources available for performance under one contract can be salvaged, but **only** if they can be **salvaged**, the fair market value of the salvaged materials must be subtracted from other damages as a "loss avoided" to calculate accurately the injured party's expectation recovery
            6. ***** Expectation Damages Formula *****
                a. **Expectation Damages = Lost Value (value of full performance – value actually received) + Incidental Loss + Consequential Loss – Cost Avoided – Loss Avoided**
    v. Examples of breaches in the most common type of non-UCC contracts:
        1. Employment Contracts: Breach by Employer
            a. The rule regarding whether salary from another job should be accounted for as a loss avoided in cases when an employer has breached an employment contract is:
                i. Any salary **actually earned** in substitute work during the time period of the original contract must be accounted for as a "loss avoided" regardless of whether it is "comparable" to the work from which the employee was unjustly terminated
                ii. If an offer of **comparable** substitute work is not accepted, any salary that **could** have been earned in such a comparable position during the time period must also be accounted for as a loss avoided
                iii. If an employee is offered **non-comparable** work that he rejects, any salary that *could* have been made at the non-comparable position does NOT have to be counted as a loss **avoided**
        2. Construction Contracts: Breach by the Builder
            a. There are **special rules governing the calculation of "lost value" in these cases**

b. The reason for the special rules has to do with the fact that there are two reasonable ways of calculating lost value in a construction contract when the builder breaches:
    i. By the diminution in fair market value of the property caused by the breach, OR
    ii. By the amount of money necessary to finish the job (if the builder never starts construction or quits part way through), or the amount of money necessary to remedy any problems with the construction (if the builder finished the work, but did not perform it well)
c. Accordingly, in a rather complicated series of rules set forth in §§347, 348, and 350, the Restatement has adopted the following rules to compute "lost value" for the breach of construction contracts where the breach is caused by the builder:
    i. **Rule No. 1**: If the diminution in the fair market value of the property caused by the breach is greater than the cost of completion or repair, the injured party may only use the cost of completion or repair as the "lost value"
    ii. **Rule No. 2**: If the cost of completion or repair is greater than the diminution in the fair market value of the property caused by the breach, the injured party is **still** *generally* entitled to the cost of completion or repair as the "lost value" [Rest. §348, Com. c].
    iii. **Rule No. 3**: When the cost of completion or repair is so much greater than the diminution in fair market value to the property caused by the breach **so that it is "clearly disproportionate"** to the amount of diminution in market value, the injured party may **only** use the decreased fair market value as the "lost value" and is not entitled to use the disproportionately greater amount of the repair or completion cost in computing expectation damages [Rest. §348(2)(b)] See ***Peevyhouse v. Garland Coal & Mining Co***
        1. Note: some authorities limit the applicability of Rule No. 3 to those

situations where the breach is non-willful

   2. Ex: ***Jacobs & Youngs, Inc. v. Kent***. The use of Cohoes pipe instead of Reading pipe did not change the fair market value of the house, whereas replacing the pipe would have been very expensive. Therefore, Kent is entitled only to the diminished fair market value of his home caused by the breach as the "lost value" component. If the breach had been willful, i.e., had Jacob & Youngs deliberately used Cohoes pipe instead of Reading, there are some authorities that would have allowed Kent to recover the full cost of repair

E. THREE LIMITATIONS ON THE RECOVERABILTY OF EXPECTATION DAMAGES: CERTAINTY, FORESEEABILITY, AND AVOIDABILITY
   i. The "Certainty" limitation. Damages may not be recovered for breach of contract, unless they are proven with "reasonable certainty"
      1. **This rule is not limited to expectation damages**, i.e., **all** contract damages must be proven with sufficient certainty to be recoverable [Rest. §352]. However, when the reasonable certainty limitation is applied to expectation damages, it is almost always in the context of denying an injured party's attempt to recover lost profits as a **consequential damage**
   ii. The "Foreseeability" limitation: Damages may not be recovered unless the breaching party either foresaw or should have foreseen at the time the contract was made that such a damage would follow from breach
      1. It is this principle which both defines consequential damages and limits the recovery of such damages
      2. The modern rule is stated in Rest. §351(1): **Damages are not recoverable for loss that the party in breach did not have reason to foresee as a probable result of the breach when the contract was made**
      3. The **difficulties** in application of the rule are of two related, but distinct types: (i) deciding *what* makes a loss sufficiently foreseeable to the party in breach so that it will be recoverable *without* a special proof of foreseeability (that is, the damage is then a direct damage and not a consequential one) and (ii) deciding *what* kind of showing

61

the injured party must make if it is determined that the injured party must make a showing of foreseeability
4. Ex: The origin of the doctrine is the most famous case in contract law, the English decision ***Hadley v. Baxendale***. An employee of the carrier Pickford & Co. (owned by Baxendale) promised two day delivery of the crankshaft to W. Joyce & Co., when in fact it took seven days. Hadley sued Baxendale for five days worth of lost profits at the mill, which he asserted was £300. **Held**: Hadley was **not** entitled to recover for the lost profits from the mill's being shut down an extra five days. He was not denied such recovery on "certainty" grounds, but on "foreseeability" grounds
5. ***Hadley*** set forth two rules regarding the recoverability of expectation damages:
    a. A non-breaching party may recover direct damages without having to prove specially that such damages were foreseeable
    b. Any damage that was not a direct damage was, by definition, a "consequential" damage. To recover consequential damages, the non-breaching party must **prove** that the breaching party either foresaw, or should have foreseen, them as following from the breach
        i. The burden was on the injured party to prove that in the case at hand there was some *notice* given the breaching party that this unusual "consequential" damage would follow from the breach of the particular contract at issue
6. The first question in deciding the case presented in ***Hadley*** was to determine whether the lost profits due to the mill's being shut down were "direct" or "consequential" damages. That is, would a loss of profits from a business having to close down production "arise naturally, according to the usual course of things" from the failure to deliver a package promptly? If so, the lost profits would be direct damages, and thereby recoverable without showing foreseeability. If not, then the loss would be consequential and thus recoverable only if Hadley had somehow put Baxendale's company on notice that a delayed delivery would result in lost profits for the mill
7. The Modern Test for Whether a Loss is "Direct" or "Consequential"
    a. **Damages are direct if they follow "in the ordinary course of events" from the breach**

62

[Rest. §351(2)(a); UCC §2-714(1)]. All other damages are consequential
- i. Generally, the only time there is any question at all regarding whether a loss was sufficiently foreseeable to be "direct" arises in **the recovery of lost profits**. However, while (virtually) all consequential losses arise upon an attempt to recover lost profits, not all lost profits are consequential losses
- ii. **The foreseeability of the loss is judged at the time the contract was made, not at the time the contract was breached**
- iii. The test of foreseeability is an **objective** one. The test is whether a **reasonable person**, looking at the contract when it was made, would have foreseen that the injured party would lose profits in the ordinary course of events if the other party breached. If so, such lost profit is a direct damage. If not, it is consequential
- iv. **It is only necessary that such loss foreseeably be a "probable result", not a certain result, of the breach**

8. The showing the non-breaching party must make to recover consequential damages under modern contract law
   a. *Hadley*: "**tacit agreement test**," which stated that consequential losses were recoverable only when the injured party could prove that **both parties** to the contract had **tacitly agreed** that the consequential losses would be recoverable upon a breach. Modern contract law has **rejected** this test
   b. "**Reason to foresee test**": The injured party must prove that, at the time of contract formation, the breaching party either *knew* or *had reason to know* that such loss would follow as a probable result of the breach. [Rest. §351(2)(b); UCC §2-715(2)(a)]
      - i. Ex: Wu purchases a brand new Dodge mini-van from a Dealer. Unknown to dealer, Wu planned to use the van in his automobile repossession business (unknown to Wu's parents was the fact that he had quit his medical residency program in plastic surgery; they think he is learning to fix up Hollywood starlets' T&A (we all know how Wu was a T&A man @ Amherst...) when in fact he motors around with a .357 magnum

by his side to protect himself against the deadbeats he encounters in his repo business). A few months after Wu purchased the van, while it is still under warranty, the van stops working (Wu is pissed off that he was suckered into buying an American hunk-o'-junk). Wu has it towed to the Dealer's, and it takes Dealer two days to find and fix the electrical problem. During the two days that Wu's minivan was in the shop, Wu cannot work, and his company **loses profits** it would have made on repossessing cars for those two days. **Held**: Wu will not be able to recover for his lost profits due to the foreseeability doctrine. That is, the lost profits suffered by Wu are not "direct" damages, for a reasonable person viewing the contract at the time it was negotiated would not foresee that if the van had electrical problems, the purchaser would probably suffer a loss of business. As a consequential loss, the lost profits can only be recovered by Wu if he somehow put the Dealer on notice so that the Dealer knew, or should have known, that one result of a breach would be that Wu would suffer lost profits

iii. The Avoidability Limitation
 1. **A party may not recover damages that it could have avoided or mitigated without undue risk, burden, or humiliation** [Rest. §350]
    a. Ex: Chris contracts to build a vacation home on property Stevie owns 1,000 miles from his principal residence. Chris promptly begins construction, but after a week he receives a telegram from Stevie unequivocally telling him to stop construction, as he has decided not to go forward with the building project. At the time Chris receives the telegram, he has spent $5,000 in labor and materials. Chris nevertheless spends another two weeks working on the house in the hopes that Stevie will change his mind. During these extra two weeks he incurs another $7,500 in labor and materials costs. The extra $7,500 is not recoverable under the avoidability doctrine, for Chris could have avoided

those damages without undue risk, burden, or humiliation

F. **RELIANCE DAMAGES**
  i. Reliance damages are designed to put the injured party in the *ex ante* position, that is, in the position the party was in before the contract was signed
  ii. The value of reliance damages is typically equal to the amount of out-of-pocket costs, including labor, incurred by the injured party at the time of the breach either in preparation for performance, actual performance, or other **foreseeable collateral expenses**, e.g. advertising, under the contract. ***Foreseeable* consequential expenses that were incurred in reliance on the contract are also recoverable**
  iii. The availability of reliance damages
    1. Reliance damages are always available to an injured party as an alternative to expectation damages [Rest. §344]
    2. Typically, however, reliance damages are sought only when the injured party is unable to prove his or her expectation damages with reasonable certainty, or when such damages are not sufficiently foreseeable to be recovered
    3. *L. Albert & Son v. Armstrong Rubber Co.* As to **consequential damages**, the owner of a plant who incurs expenses by building a foundation on which to install machinery may recover these expenses if the machines are not delivered
    4. *Security Stove & Mfg. Co. v. American Ry. Exp. Co.* Not all contracting parties contemplate a direct and identifiable profit from the contract. A manufacturer may contract to have a product shipped to a convention for display in the hopes of attracting interest in its product, rather than immediate sales. If the shipper is aware of the manufacturer's purpose, it can **foresee** that in reliance upon the contract, the manufacturer will rent exhibition space and incur other expenses. In the event of breach, such reliance expenditures are recoverable
  iv. Limitations on Reliance Damage Recovery
    1. Any damages claimed must be proven with **reasonable certainty** [Rest. §352]
      a. As a practical matter, the reasonable certainty requirement rarely serves to limit an injured party's recovery of reliance damages because reliance damages are typically valued in an amount equal to the out-of-pocket costs incurred by the injured party
    2. If the breaching party can prove that **the injured party would have lost money** on the contract if it had been

65

performed, i.e., it was a "losing contract", the amount of **the loss must be subtracted** from any reliance damage recovery [Rest. §349]
- a. It is because of this rule that a party in a losing contract will usually opt for restitutionary recovery instead of a reliance damage recovery
- b. Ex: [*L. Albert & Son v. Armstrong Rubber Co.*] Kenny contracted to build a swimming pool for Gary at a price of $35,000. About a week after Kenny began construction, Gary unjustifiably fired him. At the time of the breach, Kenny can establish he had spent $7,000 in materials and labor on the project, which Gary refuses to pay. Accordingly, Kenny files suit seeking to recover for reliance damages. During discovery, Gary obtains Kenny's internal profit and loss figures for the job. As a result, Gary can competently establish at trial that Kenny underbid the pool project and would have lost $5,000 had the project been completed. As a result, Kenny's reliance damage recovery would only be $2,000. Note, that if he were awarded the full $7,000 he has spent on reliance up to the time of the breach, he would be in a **better** position than he would have been in had the contract been performed. That is, he would be "even", whereas had the contract been performed he would have been $5,000 "in the hole". Hence, the amount of such provable losses must be subtracted from his reliance damages recovery in keeping with the general goal of contract damages

3. The **value** of any materials purchased by the non-breaching party in performance or preparation for performance that **can be salvaged must be subtracted** from any reliance damage recovery
4. Any damages claimed must **not have been avoidable** by the non-breaching party without undue burden, risk, or humiliation [Rest. §350]

v. **Recovery based on the reliance interest in other situations**
1. In certain situations, reliance is the only recovery available to the non-breaching party. These situations include:
   - a. Recovery based on promissory estoppel [Rest. §90]
   - b. Recovery based on pre-performance by the offeree that does not rise to the level of acceptance [Rest. §87(2)]

                c. Recovery based on actions taken in reliance on promises that are unenforceable under the statute of frauds [Rest. §139]
                d. Recovery based on actions taken in reliance on promises made in pre-offer, preliminary negotiations
    G. **EMOTIONAL DISTRESS DAMAGES ARE GENERALLY NOT AVAILABLE IN BREACH OF CONTRACT SUITS**
        i. There are two exceptions to the general bar on emotional distress recovery arising from a breach of contract suit:
            1. When the breach also results in tangible personal injury
                a. Ex: ***Sullivan v. O'Connor***. The court allowed Ms. Sullivan to recover for the pain and suffering and mental distress she suffered with respect to her third operation
            2. When emotional distress is **"particularly likely"** to result from breach of a specific contract [Rest. §353]
                a. Mortuary mishandles corpse
                b. Telegram mistakenly tells wrong person that loved ones have died
                c. Insurance company is guilty of "bad faith" breach
    H. **LIQUIDATED DAMAGES**
        i. Liquidate damages are damages the parties have agreed to in advance
        ii. These clauses in contracts are often not enforced:
            1. A party should not be better off as a result of a breach than he would have been had the contract been performed
            2. A party should not be *penalized* for breaching a contract [Rest. §356, Com. a]
                a. The liquidated damage clause makes it too expensive for a party to breach under the principles of efficient breach doctrine
        iii. Requirements for an enforceable liquidated damage provision
            1. That the amount of the liquidate damage is **reasonable in light of the anticipated harm** to the injured party that was foreseen at the time of the contract formation, OR that the amount is **reasonable in light of the actual harm** suffered by the injured party, AND
            2. That there is some reason to believe that there will be **difficulties in proving the actual loss with precision** [UCC §2-718(1)]
    I. ***** <u>**EXAM APPROACH TO DAMAGE ISSUES**</u> *****
        i. When one party has breached the contract, you must always discuss the amount of damages recoverable to the non-breaching party
        ii. Always look to the basic damage formula

iii. Realize that in planning your analysis that in every breach situation, you must discuss the *possibility* of reliance and restitution. That is, because a lawyer representing the plaintiff in a breach of action has the option of suing for any of these three recoveries, you must demonstrate to the Prof that you know this rule and that you will represent your future clients well. Quite often in an exam, one approach will yield a significantly higher result than the other two
iv. Make sure you realize that any *losses* the breaching party can establish must be subtracted from either expectation or reliance damages, and that certainty, foreseeability, and the absence of mitigation should always be examined when discussing damage recovery

XV. REMEDIES: RESTITUTION

A. RESTITUTION GENERALLY
i. The crux of restitution can be fairly easily stated: a person who has been *unjustly* enriched by another must account for that enrichment, usually by restoring the value of the benefits received through a payment of money
ii. **Recovery in restitution is based on the value of the enrichment received by the benefited party, and NOT on the value of the aggrieved party's promises**
   1. If the benefits received by the benefited party turn out to be worth *more* than the value of the contractual promise, then the aggrieved party may recover **more** than the value of the contractual promise, and likewise if the benefits received are worth less
iii. **Recovery in restitution is based on the value of the enrichment actually received by the benefited party, and not on the value of the efforts undertaken by the aggrieved party**
   1. Ex: If Selden contracts to build a snowboard for Sully at the cost of $2000, and after Selden has spent $1,500 in materials and labor in building the snowboard, Sully cancels, then Selden cannot recover his expenditures in restitution since he has not conferred any benefits on Sully. He can recover in reliance or expectation
   2. An award of reliance damages attempts to put the **innocent party** in the position he was in before the contract was signed. An award of restitution attempts to put a **benefited party** in the position he was in before the contract was signed. The interesting thing is that the **benefited party** can be the *innocent party* **or** the breaching party
iv. **Restitution is potentially available as a remedy for both the breaching and the non-breaching parties**

1. Because restitutionary recovery focuses only on the value of any benefits received, and not on a party's promises, it does not matter whether those benefits were received by the non-breaching party or by the breaching party. That is, as long as the non-breaching party has received unpaid-for benefits, and so long as it would be unjust for the non-breaching party to retain those benefits without paying for them, the *non-breaching* party will be liable to the breacher in restitution

B. RULES COMMON TO ALL RESTITUTION ACTIONS
   i. The value of the benefits conferred on the benefited party must be properly valued under the appropriate method
   ii. When a party seeks restitution, he must make restitution. That is, there must be mutual restitution or there can be no restitution

C. TWO COMMON METHODS OF VALUING THE RESTITUTION INTEREST: THE "COST AVOIDED" AND THE "NET BENEFIT" METHODS
   i. An important question is how the benefits received by the other party are valued
   ii. The "cost avoided" and the "net benefit" methods are two well-known ways to calculate the value of a party's benefits. Sometimes they are all you need in analyzing a restitution problem. Other times, these methods will only be a start, or you won't be given enough information to calculate the value of the benefits received under these methods. In those cases, try to come up with a fair and reasonable amount value to the benefits received
   iii. **The "Cost Avoided" method** holds that the benefits received by the benefited party should be valued as the dollar amount it would have cost the benefited party to obtain those benefits from another [Rest. §371(a)]. That is, under the cost avoided method the question is what is the fair market value of the benefits received by the benefited party, as **measured by how much it would have costs the benefited party to hire someone else to provide those benefits**
   iv. **The "Net Benefit" method** holds that the benefit to the enriched party should be valued as the dollar amount of the extent to which the benefited party's property has been increased in value, or his other interests advanced, by the actions of the aggrieved party [Rest. §371(b)]. That is, under this approach the measure of the benefits received by the enriched party is **the difference in the fair market value of his property, or his net worth, before and after the actions of the aggrieved party**
   v. If the benefit conferred by the aggrieved party is a **cash payment**, then the dollar value of the restitutionary recovery due under these two methods yields the same result

vi. Where the benefits provided are **services**, however, it is **very unlikely** the two valuation methods will yield the same results
    1. Ex: Wagner hired Julio to build a custom home for him. Julio timely began construction and had done quite a bit of work on the house when Wagner breached and ordered him off his property. Julio brings suit against Wagner seeking to recover for his restitutionary interest. Competent evidence will show that the reasonable value of the work performed by Julio was $70,000 at the time of the breach, and that the market value of Wagner's property increased by $30,000 as a result of having a partially completed structure on it.
    2. Using the "cost avoided" method, Julio's actions benefited Wagner by $70,000, for this is the amount it would have cost him to hire someone else to provide those benefits, and thus it is also the *cost* he *avoided* by not having to pay someone else for those services
    3. Using the "net benefit" method, however, Julio benefited Wagner by only $30,000, for this figure constitutes the extent to which the fair market value of his property increased by Julio's actions
vii. Determining which method of valuing the restitution interest should be used in ascertaining an aggrieved party's restitutionary recovery
    1. The court has complete discretion on which method to use depending on which one seems the most "just" in that particular situation. However, contract law has developed presumptions as to which method should be used:
        a. When a **non-breaching party is seeking restitutionary recovery against the breacher**, the presumption is that the non-breaching party will be entitled to recover using the method which yields **the most generous recovery** [Rest. §371, Com. b]
        b. **A *willful* breacher cannot recover in restitution at all** under the *majority* rule. Note that a non-willful breacher, i.e., someone who may ultimately be adjudged a breacher but who has a colorable and good faith reason for not performing, and, in a *minority* of jurisdictions, even a willful breacher, does have the right to sue for restitutionary relief
        c. In those situations that allow it, when a **breaching party is seeking restitutionary recovery against a non-breacher**, the presumption is that the breaching party will be entitled to recover using the method that yields **the least generous recovery** [Rest. §374, Com. b]

D. THE "MUTUAL RESTITUTION" REQUIREMENT
  i. An aggrieved party who seeks restitution of a benefit he has conferred on another must offer to return whatever benefits he has received from the other party as part of final restitutionary judgment [Rest. §384]
    1. Ex: Mani hires Farra to build an addition onto his house. Under their contract, Mani was obligated to make monthly progress payments to Farra. Farra began construction and had both laid the foundation and put up two walls when Mani unjustly fired him. At that point, Mani had paid Farra $15,000 in monthly progress payments. To be entitled to sue Mani in restitution, Farra will have to offer to return the $15,000 in progress payments under the rule of [Rest. §384(1)], and will have to be prepared to pay that money, or at least account for it as an offset, in any restitutionary recovery
    2. Ex: Same as above, except this time it was Farra who breached, and Mani sued Farra in restitution for the $15,000 progress payments. Obviously, Mani could not "return" the foundation and the walls. In cases like this where return of the exact benefits provided by the breaching party is either impossible or unavailing, the aggrieved party must at least offer to offset the value of such benefits in any restitutionary recovery [Rest. §384(2)]
  ii. Limitations on the availability of restitution as a remedy for breach of contract
    1. Restitution is only available if the injured party would be able to sue the breaching party for total, opposed to partial, breach [Rest. §373, Com. a]
      a. Ex: Anthony contracts to network a house for Gordon for $100,000, progress payments to be made monthly. The contract called for Nortel cables to be used. After having been paid $40,000 for two months, Anthony commits a breach that is not material by inadvertently using Cisco cables. Gordon has a claim for damages for partial breach but cannot recover the $40,000 that he has paid Anthony
    2. A party injured by the other's breach is **not** entitled to restitution if he has performed all of his duties under the contract, and the only remaining performance due under the agreement by the breaching party is payments of a **definite sum of money** [Rest. §373(2)]
      a. Where a supplier's expectation damages can be so easily calculated with reference to the contract price, there is no need to resort to restitution

      b. Ex: Keyser has agreed to paint a portrait of Dub for $7,000. Keyser paints the portrait and timely delivers it to Dub, who keeps it but refuses to pay for it. Keyser is not entitled to restitution even though Dub will be unjustly enriched if he fails to pay for it. That is because Keyser (the non-breaching party), has performed all of his duties under the contract, and the only performance remaining is for Dub (the breacher) to pay a fixed sum of money. As such, Keyser must sue to recover the contract price as part of his expectation damages. This is exactly the kind of case where the court should not be burdened with trying to decide the value of the painting, i.e., the objective value of the benefit Keyser has conferred on Dub, when the parties themselves established that value when they made the contract, and where the extent of Keyser's expectation loss is so easily calculable from the contract price

      c. Ex: As he is prone to do when drunk, Bart brags to Steven that he can paint better than Rembrandt. Steven does not know that Bart is full of b.s. as usual, and contracts with him to paint his portrait for $100,000. Steven makes the payment, but Bart tenders a painting resembling finger painting. Steven is entitled to recover $100,000 in restitution. In this case, Steven has fully performed all of his duties under the contract. He is not barred restitutionary recovery because Bart's remaining duty is to deliver a painting "worthy of Rembrandt", which is a good, not a fixed sum of money. Accordingly, Steven would be entitled to the value of the benefit he conferred on Bart, in this case $100,000

E. SOME TYPICAL SITUATIONS WHEN THE NON-BREACHING PARTY SEEKS A RESTITUTIONARY RECOVERY FROM THE BREACHER

    i. Losing Contract Situation

        1. Ex: James is hired to construct an office building on Gregory's property for $1 million. James starts construction in a timely fashion and spent $600,000 in labor and materials when Gregory breaches by telling him to stop. Internal profit and loss documents show that James would have needed to spend another $500,000 to finish construction. The reasonable value of James's services was $600,000 for that is the amount most other contractors in

the area are prepared to testify that they would have charged to perform the services James did before the breach. The market value of Gregory's property increased by $350,000 as a result of the partially constructed building
2. In a suit for breach, James would not sue for expectation or reliance damages since he underbid the contract and would have lost $100,000 on it. In reliance or expectation he would be awarded $500,000. James would sue under restitution, and be awarded $600,000 under the cost avoided method, since it is greater than $350,000 under the net benefit method

ii. When the value of the benefits provided exceeds the contract price
1. Ex: Arjun hires Sebastian to paint his house for $800. Sebastian has almost finished when Arjun fires him. As this was Sebastian's first commercial painting job, he priced his services well under market. Most other painters in the area would have charged at least $1,500 for doing the work Sebastian did before the breach, and his efforts in almost completely painting Arjun's house have increased its market value by $1,000
    a. Sebastian would seek restitution against Arjun for his breach. This is because, once again, **restitution only focuses on the value of the benefits received, not on the value of a party's promised performance**. Hence, the contract price does **not** provide a ceiling for restitutionary recovery, and so Sebastian is entitled to recover for the **value** of the enrichment his services provided to Arjun. As he is the non-breaching party seeking restitution, he is presumptively entitled to the greater of the amounts calculated under the cost avoided or net benefit methods
    b. Under the cost avoided method, the amount of benefits received by Arjun is $1,500, for that is the cost Arjun avoided by not having to pay another painter to do the work Sebastian did
    c. Under the net benefit method, the value of the services retained by Arjun was $1,000, for that is the net increase in the fair market value of Arjun's property caused by Sebastian's services
    d. Hence, Sebastian will recover $1,500 in restitution for the breach of a contract for which he would have only been paid $800 had it been performed
    e. Note: If Arjun had waited until Sebastian had finished, and then simply not paid him, Sebastian would **not** have been entitled to sue in restitution

for the value of his services; he would have been limited by the contract price
   iii. When the value of the benefits is less than the contract price
        1. Ex: Barry has a contract to build a custom-made wall unit for Danny's stereo system. He is to build it in place at Danny's house. The contract price is $3,500. Barry timely began construction and is partially completed when Danny breaches and orders him to stop. At that point Barry has spent $2,000 in labor and materials, and his partially constructed wall unit has increased the value of Danny's home by $300. It turns out that Barry is an expensive carpenter for the area, as most other carpenters would charge only $1,750 to do the work Barry did prior to the breach
           a. Barry's restitutionary recovery would be limited to $1,750. This is, once again, because recovery in restitution focuses only on the value of the benefits received by the other party, and not on the cost to provide those benefits
           b. Obviously, under these facts Barry would prefer suing at least for his reliance, if not for his expectation damages

F. SOME TYPICAL SITUATIONS WHEN THE BREACHING PARTY SEEKS A RESTITUTIONARY RECOVERY FROM THE NON-BREACHER
   i. Requirements for breaching parties to seek recovery in restitution
      1. None of the special rules that govern whether a non-breacher can sue in restitution apply for a breaching party instituting such a suit
      2. Hence, so long as the breaching party offers to restore any benefits he has received under the contract as part of the final restitution, and so long as the party is a non-willful breacher or is in the minority of jurisdictions allowing all breaching parties to sue, such a claim can be brought
   ii. Calculating the value of the restitutionary award in cases brought by the breaching party
      1. The value of the benefits received by the non-breaching party must be calculated on both a "cost avoided" and a "net benefit" basis
      2. There is a presumption that the method yielding the **least generous valuation** measure should be used for the breaching party [Rest. §374, Com. b]
      3. Because it is the breaching party who is seeking recovery, any damages suffered by the non-breacher **must then be subtracted** from the value of the benefits received by the

non-breacher to arrive at the proper amount for the breaching party's restitutionary award

4. **That is, calculation of the breacher's recovery in these cases is a two-step process**
   a. The value of the service received by the non-breaching party must be calculated, and the least generous measure is presumptively selected
   b. From that value, the amount of any losses the non-breaching party suffered due to the breach must be subtracted to arrive at the proper net restitutionary award
5. Ex: Lennox is in the business of making repairs to office buildings damaged by fire. He contracts to repair a commercial building that was severely damaged for a price of $60,000, which is to be paid on completion of the work. Lennox works on the building for a few weeks, reasonably incurring $20,000 in labor and material costs. At trial, it can be established that other builders in the area would have charged a similar amount to perform the services provided by Lennox up to the point of the breach. However, Lennox breaches and leaves the work site to take another, more lucrative job. The owner of the building hired someone to replace Lennox, who finished the repairs for $45,000. In addition, since it took a week longer to finish the clean-up due to the delay in finding Lennox's replacement, the building owner lost $2,000 in rent. Cleaning up the building from the fire damage increased its fair market value by $55,000
   a. The building owner would likely not bring suit against Lennox, for he only had to spend $45,000 (plus $2,000 in lost rent) to get the benefits of a job for which he had contracted to pay Lennox $60,000
   b. However, Lennox will bring suit, for he has received nothing for the benefits provided the owner. Because Lennox is the breaching party, he can only sue in restitution
   c. The next issue is to determine the value of the benefits he provided the building owner:
      i. Under the cost avoided method, Lennox provided $20,000 in benefits (cost others would have charged to provide those same services)
      ii. Under the net benefit method, the value received from the landowner from Lennox's efforts was only $10,000

1. The clean up increased the building's value by $55,000
2. The $55,000 increase in fair market value was a result of the work of both Lennox and his replacement
3. We know that the services of Lennox's replacement were worth $45,000, and so the net benefit to the landowner of Lennox's work in repairing the building would be $55,000 minus $45,0000, which is $10,000

iii. Because Lennox is the breaching party, he is presumptively limited to using the valuation method yielding the least generous amount of recovery, or $10,000

iv. In addition, the $2,000 lost rent suffered by the landowner must also be subtracted from Lennox's recovery, so the net restitutionary relief due to Lennox is **$8,000**

v. Note that Lennox will consider this unfair since he is out-of-pocket $20,000 in labor and materials. However, as the breaching party, contract law believes he should not be heard complaining about receiving the least generous measure of recovery. In other words, **he could have ensured that the deal went forward**. When he chose to breach, one of the consequences he had to suffer was the least generous method of restitutionary recovery for his work thus far

G. ***** <u>EXAM APPROACH TO RESTITUTION ISSUES</u> *****
   i. Every time you are expected to discuss damages for breach of contract, you must also consider, and likely discuss restitutionary relief as well
   ii. Recall that restitution is always available to the non-breaching party (subject to limitations), and is often, but not always, available to the breaching party as well. Remember also that a party who decides to seek restitution must return any benefits he received under the contract to the other party
   iii. If you decide that recovery in restitution is available, recall that the amount of the recovery is dependant on the value of the benefits actually received by the other party. The only "fixed" rule for determining the value of restitutionary recovery is that the result be just and reasonable, but typically courts look to the "**cost avoided**"

and "**net benefit**" methods at least as a starting point in calculating those benefits

XVI. REMEDIES: REMEDIES FOR BREACH UNDER THE UCC

    A. UCC REMEDIES GENERALLY
        i. The remedies for breach of contract governed by Article 2 of the UCC do not differ in kind from the types of equitable relief, money damages, and restitution remedies discussed already

    B. EQUITABLE REMEDIES AVAILABLE TO BUYERS
        i. There are two equitable remedies specifically available to the non-breaching buyer under UCC §2-716: (1) specific performance and (2) replevin
        ii. Specific Performance [UCC §2-716(1)]
            1. The court may order specific performance "where the goods are unique **or in other proper circumstances**"
            2. Case law has established that a court should order specific performance under §2-716(1) whenever it would be "**unreasonably burdensome**" to require the buyer to locate and acquire comparable goods upon a breach

    C. BUYER'S RIGHT TO SUE FOR DAMAGES IN CASES WHERE HE DOES NOT HAVE THE GOODS
        i. This section covers the Code's treatment of those situations in which a non-breaching buyer sues the breaching seller for damages where the buyer does not have the goods. There are three reasons why a non-breaching buyer may not have the goods when a suit for breach is filed:
            1. The seller breached by never tendering the goods to the buyer
            2. The buyer rightfully and effectively rejected non-conforming goods provided by the seller, and the seller breached by not adequately curing
            3. The buyer rightfully and effectively revoked his acceptance of non-conforming goods provided by the seller, and the seller breached by not adequately curing
        ii. In these cases, the UCC provides the buyer with two related, but distinct remedies:
            1. The buyer can go into the market, purchase replacement goods ("cover"), and sue for the difference between the cover price and the contract price, along with other related damages [UCC §2-712], OR
            2. The buyer can choose not to purchase replacement goods, and instead simply sue for the difference between the market price (i.e., the price pending if the buyer had covered) and the contract price, along with other related damages [UCC §2-713]

iii. UCC §2-712: Cover Damages
   1. A buyer who ends up without goods due to a seller's breach is entitled to go in the market and "cover" by purchasing substitute goods. If the cost of cover is more than the contract price, the buyer is entitled to sue the breaching seller for that price differential
      a. A party is allowed to effect "**reasonable** cover" by acting in "good faith and without unreasonable delay"
      b. Accordingly, the idea of cover in UCC §2-712(1) allows the non-breaching buyer some flexibility in proceeding after a breach. **Rather than having his damages fixed on the day of the breach** as the difference between market price for identical goods pending that day and the contract price, the buyer is entitled to spend some time looking for reasonably comparable goods. So long as the buyer acts reasonably and in good faith in purchasing replacement goods, he is entitled to recover the full amount of his cover damages
      c. ** Formula for Recovery of Cover Damages **
         i. **Buyer's Cover Damages = [(Cost of Cover) – (Contract Price)] + Incidental Damages + Consequential Damages – Costs Avoided as a Consequence of the Breach**
         ii. In addition to cover damages under §2-712, **a buyer in these types of cases is also entitled to recover any money he has already paid to the breaching seller as part of a down payment, deposit, etc.** [UCC §2-711(1)]
            1. Ex: Best Buy placed an order with Billy's electronics for 100 single disc CD players at $200 each. Billy's breaches the contract. Best Buy's CEO spends 10 hours on the phone trying to find replacement units. He finally locates 100 5-disc CD players at $207 each, and has them expressed shipped to his store. The express shipping cost $400 more than regular freight shipment. One of the reasons he used express shipping is that he was out of stock of CD players, and already had lost two

sales. At trial, he can prove the he could have sold the players for $350 each to the two buyers. Also, he can prove that a fair value of his time is $30/hour
        a. Cover Price: 100 units x $207/unit = $20,700
        b. Contract Price: 100 units x $200/unit = $20,000
        c. Incidental Damages: A buyer's incidental damages under the Code are governed by §2-715(1) and are defined the same way as in non-UCC contracts. Accordingly, Best Buy can recover for two types of incidental loss:
            i. Labor: 10 hours x $30/hour = $300
            ii. Shipping: $400 extra
        d. Consequential Loss: Best Buy lost two sales due to Billy's breach. The profits on those units were ($350 - $200) or $150 each. This loss was plainly foreseeable, for if a seller does not provide a **retail** store with merchandise, it is certainly foreseeable that the store can lose sales. Hence, Best Buy also has $300 in recoverable consequential damages
        e. Costs Avoided: There are no costs avoided
        f. Accordingly, Best Buy's recovery under §2-712 would be: [($20,700) – ($20,000)] + $700 +300 - $0 = **$1,700**

  iv. UCC §2-713: Market Differential Damages
      1. Actually going into the market and covering may be a hassle for the non-breaching buyer
      2. UCC §2-713 holds that the buyer may avoid that hassle by suing for the difference between the fair market price of replacement goods and the contract price, together with associated other damages

3. ***** Formula for Recovery of Market Differential Damages *****
    a. **Buyer's Market Differential Damages = [(Market Price of the Goods) – (Contract Price of the Goods)] + Incidental Damages + Consequential Damages – Costs Avoided Due to the Breach**
    b. In addition to market differential damages under §2-713, **a buyer in these types of cases is also entitled to recover any money he has already paid to the breaching seller as part of a down payment, deposit, etc.** [UCC §2-711(1)]
4. Determining the "Market Price"
    a. §2-713(1) states that the temporal market price that should be used in the formula is the market price pending **"at the time the buyer learned of the breach"** (NOT the price on the day delivery was due)
    b. §2-713(2) provides that the proper geographical market price to be used depends on the nature of the seller's breach:
        i. If the seller breaches by **never tendering** goods, the "market price" is the one pending *at the place for tender*
        ii. If the seller breaches by tendering **non-conforming** goods, and the buyer rightfully either rejects or revokes his acceptance of them, then the "market price" that should be used is the *one pending at the place where the goods arrived*
        iii. Ex: Robbie, a retail buyer in California, ordered 1000 dozen grade AA eggs from a seller in New York. The contract price was $10/dozen. Under their contract, tender of the eggs was to take place in New York on May 15. Hence, Robbie planned to hire a carrier to pick up the eggs on that day in New York and transport them to California. If the contract had gone forward, the eggs were scheduled to be delivered to Robbie on May 18. On May 15, however, the seller calls Robbie and tells him that he will not deliver. The fair market value for such eggs on May 15 was $10.50/dozen in New York and $11/dozen in California. On May 18, the expected date of delivery in California, the

market value for the eggs was back to $10/dozen in New York, and it was $10.75/dozen in California
1. If Robbie chooses **not** to cover, he is entitled to recover market differential damages
2. Robbie must use the $10.50/dozen price pending in New York on May 15 in determining his market differential damages
3. Robbie's recovery is:
   a. Market Price: $10.50/dozen x 1000 dozen = $10,500
   b. Contract Price: $10/dozen x 1,000 dozen = $10,000
   c. There were no Incidental, Consequential, or Costs Avoided
   d. Accordingly, Robbie's recovery is [($10,500) – ($10,000)] = **$500**

D. BUYER'S RIGHT TO DAMAGES UPON BREACH OF GOODS HE KEEPS: WARRANY DAMAGES
   i. A buyer is entitled to accept non-conforming goods and still bring an action against the seller based on the extent to which he is economically injured by the non-conformity
   ii. Similarly, a buyer may at some point discover that he has the right to revoke his acceptance of the goods, and decide not to exercise it
   iii. Nevertheless, the buyer is still entitled to sue the seller for the difference in value between the good he was promised and the good he received
   iv. These type of cases, i.e., where the buyer decides to keep non-conforming goods and sue the seller for the diminished value of the goods due to their non-conformity, are breach of warranty claims, the damages for which are governed by UCC §2-714
   v. Once a party accepts a good, he is liable for its full contract price [UCC §2-607(1)]. Hence, in breach of warranty cases, the buyer is liable to the seller for the full contract price, but is entitled to sue the seller for the difference between the value of the conforming good he was promised and the non-conforming good he decided to keep
   vi. ***** Formula for Breach of Warranty under UCC §2-714 *****
       1. **Buyer's Warranty Damages = [(Value of Goods as Warranted) – (Value of Goods Received)] + Incidental Damages + Consequential Damages**

a. The difference between the value of goods as promised and the value of goods received
   i. The focus of the recovery is on the fair market **value** of the goods as promised and as received, and **not on the contract price**
      1. As a result, it is entirely possible that a buyer's recovery in warranty can be **greater** than the contract price he is obligated to pay the seller upon the decision to accept the good
      2. Ex: Gary is told by a sales rep at Best Buy that the TV he is thinking of buying is 8K compatible. Accordingly, Gary buys the TV for $6,000. At home, he discovers the TV is not 8K compatible
         a. Subsequent investigation establishes that a 8K compatible TV would cost $17,000
         b. Similarly most stores would charge no more than $4,000 for a TV with the features that Gary has
         c. Assuming he decides to keep the TV, the value differential which Gary is entitled under §2-714(2) is $17,000 - $4,000 or $13,000, i.e., the **value** of the TV he was promised minus the **value** of the TV he actually received
         d. Accordingly, Gary is still obligated to pay the purchase price of $6,000 because he has accepted rather than rejected or revoked acceptance of the TV, under §2-607(1), he is also entitled to at least a $13,000 warranty recovery from the store plus any incidental or consequential damages he can establish
   ii. The value differential portion of the §2-714 formula for recovery of breach of warranty

damages is often measured by the **cost to repair** the non-conforming good
   b. Consequential Damages under the UCC [§2-715]
      i. §2-715 divides consequential loss into two types, consequential economic loss and consequential personal injury and personal property loss. The chief difference between these two types of consequential loss is in the level of **foreseeability** the buyer must prove before he is entitled to their recovery
         1. The foreseeability rules governing the recovery of consequential **economic** loss under the Code are identical to the foreseeability rules for the recovery of consequential damages under common law contract principles based on *Hadley v. Baxendale*:
            a. **"Reason to foresee test"**: The injured party must prove that, at the time of contract formation, the breaching party either *knew* or *had reason to know* that such loss would follow as a probable result of the breach. [UCC §2-715(2)(a)]
         2. To recover for consequential personal injury or property loss under the Code, however, the buyer need only show that such losses **"proximately resulted"** from any breach of warranty
            a. This foreseeability test is NOT the fairly stringent foreseeability standard required in contract law, but rather the far more lenient foreseeability test of **tort law**, i.e., was the breach a proximate cause of the damage?
      ii. The **injury to the good itself is considered economic loss**. [UCC §2-715(2)]
   c. Offset of Damages under UCC §2-717

  i. Ex: Barney buys a Sony TV for $400. When the TV is delivered to his house he discovers it is a Vizio that sells for $350. Barney decides to keep the TV and pocket the extra $50. When the bill comes he is charged $400, i.e., was charged the price for the set he ordered, not the one he received
  ii. Under the rules of §2-607(1) and §2-714, Barney would be obligated to pay the store the full $400 contract price, but then would be entitled to sue the store in small claims court for the difference between the value of the goods he was promised ($400), and the value of the good he received ($350)
  iii. Since such a two step process is inefficient, under UCC §2-717 a buyer is entitled to deduct from the purchase price all or any part of the damages due the buyer resulting from the seller's breach, as long as the buyer gives adequate notice of his intentions
  iv. Accordingly, Barney is entitled to pay the store only $350 in response to its $400 bill, so long as he explains why he is doing so
E. **SELLER'S RIGHT TO SUE FOR THE FULL CONTRACT PRICE UPON BUYER'S BREACH: SELLERS "SPECIFIC PERFORMANCE"**
 i. The Code provides that a seller is entitled to bring an **action for the price (i.e. specific performance)** in only four cases:
  1. When the buyer has **accepted** the goods [UCC §2-709(1)(a)]
   a. One of the consequences of acceptance under the Code is that a buyer must pay for the contract price for goods when he accepts them [UCC §2-607(1)]. So when a party accepts goods and does not pay for them, the seller is entitled to bring an action for the full contract price [UCC §2-709(1)(a)]
   b. Note that the seller has the right to sue for the contract price regardless of whether the buyer keeps the conforming goods he has accepted, or whether the buyer ships them back to the seller. If the buyer does ship the goods back to the seller, there are two consequences:
    i. In addition to the purchase price, the buyer will also be liable for storage and other incidental expenses incurred by the seller as long as he cares for the goods [UCC §§ 2-703; 2-710] AND

ii. The buyer has implicitly given the seller permission to sell the goods for a reasonable price. So at any time before the satisfaction of a final judgment in such a case, the seller is entitled to sell the goods to another for a reasonable price. Upon such a sale, any proceeds must be credited to the breaching buyer, meaning that the damages for which the buyer is liable must be reduced by the amount of the re-sale
2. When the seller sends conforming goods to the buyer **after the risk of loss has passed to the buyer**, and when the goods are thereafter lost or destroyed before acceptance [UCC §2-709(1)(a)]
    a. When goods are shipped, at some point they become the buyer's responsibility. That is, if they are lost or destroyed during transit, the buyer must nevertheless pay for goods he has not received because he bears their "risk of loss"
    b. UCC §2-709(1)(a) codifies this concept and provides that if a buyer refuses to pay for goods that are lost or destroyed after the buyer has assumed the risk of loss, the seller is entitled to sue the buyer for the full contract price
3. **When the seller reasonably tries to re-sell the goods** to another after the buyer's breach, **but is unable to re-sell them for a reasonable price** [UCC §2-709(1)(b)]
    a. Suppose a seller tenders absolutely conforming goods to the buyer, but the buyer nevertheless breaches by rejecting the goods and returns them to the seller. At that point the buyer is not obligated to pay the purchase price for the goods, for there has been no acceptance of them [UCC §2-607(1)]. Further, normal principles of avoidability dictate that the seller try to re-sell the goods to another, thereby reducing the buyer's damages
    b. Sometimes, though, a seller will make reasonable effort to re-sell merchandise, but will not be able to find anyone willing to pay a reasonable price for the goods. This often happens when the good involved is custom-made. In such cases, when a seller is unable to re-sell wrongfully rejected goods for a reasonable price after reasonable efforts to do so, the seller is entitled to sue the buyer for the full contract price [UCC §2-709(1)(b)]

4. **When the seller does not attempt to re-sell the goods** to another after the buyer's breach **because such efforts will be unavailing** [UCC §2-709(1)(b)]
    a. Every once in a while, a good ordered specifically for a particular buyer is so unusual that a reasonable person would conclude that any attempt to re-sell it to another would be unavailing. If the seller can establish that the buyer wrongfully rejected such a good, and can carry the burden of proof to establish that any efforts to re-sell the goods would be unavailing, the seller is entitled to bring an action for the full purchase price [UCC §2-709(1)(b)]

F. SELLER'S RIGHT TO SUE FOR DAMAGES OTHER THAN THE FULL CONTRACT PRICE UPON BUYER'S BREACH
   i. Recovery under §2-706: Seller's "Cover" Damages
       1. UCC §2-706 permits a seller to re-sell the goods and thereafter be entitled to recover from the breaching buyer the difference, if any, between the re-sale price and the contract price. Since this procedure is analogous in many respects to the non-breaching buyer's right to cover under UCC §2-712, recovery under §2-706 is sometimes referred to as "seller's cover."
           a. ***** Formula For Calculating a Seller's "Cover" Damages *****
               i. Under UCC §2-706(1), when the seller has re-sold goods wrongfully rejected by the buyer and has done so in good faith and in a commercially reasonable manner [see UCC §§2-706(2) to 2-706(4)], he is entitled to damages computed as follows:
               ii. **Seller's Cover Damages=[(Contract Price for the Goods) – (Re-Sale Price for the Goods)] + Incidental Damages**
               iii. A seller's recoverable incidental damages are governed by UCC §2-710. Like other types of incidental damages, recoverable incidental losses under §2-710 are expenses incurred by the seller, after the buyer's breach, in an attempt to preserve the goods or otherwise mitigate the buyer's loss. So they include costs incurred in stopping delivery, storage charges until the goods are sold, out-of-pocket costs associated with the re-sale, etc.
               iv. Note that there is no provision for recovery of consequential loss in the §2-706 formula.

                    If a seller is claiming such loss, i.e., a lost profit resulting from the buyer's breach, the seller must proceed under §2-708(2).
                v. Ex: Manufacturer has contracted to sell 1000 Bluray players to Retailer for $200/unit. The players are timely delivered and are conforming, but Retailer nevertheless rejects. Manufacturer pays to have the players shipped back to its plant, and one of its employees spends a good deal of time trying to find a substitute buyer, which he finally does. The substitute buyer is willing, in good faith and after notice to Retailer, to purchase the players at $190/unit, a commercially reasonable price given the circumstances
                vi. Held: Under §2-706(1), Manufacturer is entitled to recover ($200/unit) – ($190/unit) x 1000 units, plus whatever incidental costs it incurred in shipping the goods back to its factory, the time spent by its employee in arranging the re-sale, and any other costs associated with the re-sale
        ii. Recovery under §2-708(1): Seller's Market Differential Damages.
            1. Just as a non-breaching buyer who chooses not to bear the costs of cover is still entitled to recover market differential damages upon a seller's breach (see UCC §2-713), a non-breaching seller is also entitled to choose not to re-sell wrongfully rejected goods and recover instead for market differential damages. Under §2-708(1), upon a buyer's wrongful rejection or repudiation a seller may recover the difference between the contract price and the market price for the goods, along with other associated damages
            2. ***** Formula for Calculating a Seller's Market Differential Damages *****
                a. **Seller's Damages=[(Contract Price for the Goods) – (Market Price for the Goods)] + Incidental Damages**
            3. Note there is no provision for the recovery of consequential loss in §2-708(1). A seller seeking lost profits as a result of the buyer's breach must proceed under §2-708(2)
            4. Determining the "Market Price"
                a. The rule is that the "market price" for the purposes of the formula is always **the market price pending at the time and place for tender** regardless of when the seller learned of the breach

- b. Ex: Alcoa, a manufacturer of aluminum cans in CA, contracts to sell 100,000 cans at $0.20/can to Food Co., at Food Co.'s Cleveland, OH plant. Under their contract, tender of the cans was to take place in CA on May 1, and delivery was expected in Cleveland on May 5. Due to worldwide economic uncertainty, the price of aluminum is fluctuating. On April 25, Food Co. breached by canceling its order and telling Alcoa not to bother tendering the cans, for no one would be there to pick them up. Alcoa had already finished making the cans. On May 1, the date of expected tender under the contract, the fair market value of aluminum cans was $0.17/can in Cleveland and $0.16/can in CA. On May 5, the date of expected delivery under the contract, the value of aluminum cans was $0.14/can in Cleveland and $0.15/can in CA
- c. Held: In determining its §2-708(1) damages, Alcoa must use the market price of the cans pending at the time and place for tender. Hence, it must use the $0.16/can price that was pending in CA on May 1, i.e., the date and place where tender was to take place under the contract. Hence, Alcoa's damages under §2-708(1) would be 20 cent/can – 16 cents/can x 100,000 cans, plus any incidental damages it can establish

iii. Recovery under §2-708(2): Seller's Lost Profit Recovery
1. A seller is entitled to recover under UCC §2-708(2), "if the measure of damages provided in [§2-708(1)] is inadequate to put the seller in as good a position as performance would have done." Then the seller's measure of damages is the "profit the seller would have made from full performance by the buyer, together with any incidental damages due allowance for costs reasonably incurred and due credit for payment or proceeds of resale"
2. Recovery of Profits for "Lost Volume" Sellers
    - a. The idea behind the "lost volume" doctrine stems from the fact that sometimes a seller is not made whole even by selling a wrongfully rejected good to another for its full contract price. This occurs when seller has an **excess supply** of goods that were the subject of the breached contract, and thus, the buyer's breach has really cost the seller a profit from a lost second sale
    - b. ***** Formula for lost volume seller's recovery of lost profits under UCC §2-708(2) ***** [Note that it

88

is accepted that there is a drafting error in §2-708(2) which is now ignored]
- c. **Seller's Damages = The *Profit* from the contract that was breached + Incidental Damages + Costs reasonably incurred in performance**

G. LIQUIDATED DAMAGES UNDER ARTICLE 2
  i. Liquidated damages are damages, the amount of which the parties have agreed in advance that will be owed upon a breach of their contract. The ability of the parties to agree to an enforceable liquidated damage provision under the Code is governed by UCC §2-718(1). The rules of §2-718(1), though, are the same as those governing the enforceability of liquidated damages clauses in non-UCC agreements: The parties' agreement on liquidated damages will only be enforced if the amount of the liquidated damages is reasonable in light of the anticipated or actual harm caused by the breach, and where the actual amount of damages is difficult to ascertain with precision

H. EMOTIONAL DISTRESS DAMAGES, PUNITIVE DAMAGES, AND RECOVERY OF PRE-JUDGMENT INTEREST UNDER THE UCC
  i. The Code has no special rules governing the recovery of emotional distress damages, punitive damages, and pre-judgment interest

I. LIMITATION ON, OR MODIFICATION OF, CONTRACT REMEDIES
  i. Under the principles of freedom of contract, UCC §2-719 provides that contracting parties of roughly equal bargaining power may validly modify the remedies for breach provided in the Code. They may even eliminate them entirely should they choose to do so. But the general rule is subject to two limitations:
    1. The parties' ability to substitute liquidated damages for the remedies of the Code is limited by the rule set forth in §§2-718(1) and 2-719(1), AND
    2. Limitation of consequential damages for injury to the person is *prima facie* unconscionable [UCC §2-719(3)]
      a. Note, however that UCC §2-719 provides that a limitation on **economic** consequential loss is **not** presumptively unconscionable, and is, in fact, specifically permitted by the Code
  ii. When a limited remedy "fails of its essential purpose" under UCC §2-719(2): Repair or Replacement Clauses.
    1. Repair or replacement clauses are common and are expressly permitted by the Code [UCC §2-719(1)(b)]. They limit and modify the otherwise-applying remedies available for breach
    2. If a buyer agrees to the repair or replacement clause as an **exclusive** remedy, he has lost the benefit of being able to resort to any other Code-based remedy should the seller breach by tendering a good that needs repairs. For the

benefit of getting the seller's repair promise, a buyer has traded his rights to seek all other Code-based relief
3. But UCC §2-719(2) provides that if the good requiring repair is never fixed despite numerous attempts at repair by the seller, the buyer is entitled to sue the seller under **any** Article 2-provided remedy despite having agreed to the repair or replacement clause. §2-719(2) provides that whenever an exclusive or limited damage provision "**fails of its essential purpose**," the buyer is thereafter entitled to recover under **any** provision of Article 2

iii. When a "No Consequential Damages" clause is linked with a "Repair or Replacement" Clause
1. Another recurring issue in commercial transactions under §2-719 is what happens when there is not just one limitation of remedy clause, but two
2. Ex: Suppose Doug's machine shop had a contract to sell a computerized drill press to Andy's manufacturing plant. In their contract, there is **both** an exclusive repair or replacement clause, **and** a limitation on Andy's ability to collect consequential damages upon a breach. Once again, assume there has been a failure of the essential purpose of the repair and replacement clause, as Doug has not fixed a recurring problem with the press
    a. The issue is whether the breach of one limited damage provision acts as a breach of both of them, or whether the breach of the repair and replacement clause is independent of the consequential damages limitation. That is, if there were only a repair and replacement clause, when it failed of its essential purpose Andy would be entitled to recovery under any UCC provision, including ones allowing for consequential loss [§2-719(2)]
    b. However, in his contract Andy also agreed to a consequential damage limitation. Hence, Doug would argue that breach of the repair and replacement clause means that Andy is entitled to recover under any UCC provision **except** those allowing for recovery of consequential damages. He will say that Andy separately agreed that he would **never** be liable for such damages under their contract when he agreed to the consequential damage limitation clause. Andy, on the other hand, would argue that the clauses were linked, i.e., that they are dependent on each other. He would allege that the only reason he agreed to the consequential damage limitation is because Doug had provided a

repair or replacement guarantee. Hence, his view would be that the breach of the repair or replacement promise should also render the consequential damage limitation unenforceable
- c. It is fair to say there is no uniform treatment of this issue by the courts. Increasingly, however, courts are seeking to discover the parties' true intentions in agreeing to these clauses, i.e., did the parties consider them dependent or independent:
    - i. If a court finds that the parties intended to link them together, then breach of the repair or replacement provision will also result in the breach of the consequential damages limitation as well, and someone as Andy can thus recover for his provable consequential loss
    - ii. If the parties intended for the clauses to be independent, then they will be interpreted independently. In such a case, Doug's breach of the repair or replacement promise will not effect the consequential damage limitation and will thus supercede the effect of §2-719(2)
- iv. Distinction between limitation of remedy under UCC §2-719 and Disclaimer of Warranty under UCC §2-316
    1. When the clause in question **completely eliminates the warranty** so that it is impossible to breach that kind of warranty under the contract, the clause is a **warranty disclaimer** and **UCC §2-316's provisions govern**
    2. However, if a contract provision provides that a breach of warranty can still occur, but that the *range of remedies for such breach is limited*, e.g., instead of a lawsuit the buyer is limited to repair or replacement remedy, then the *rules of §2-719 are operative*

J. ***** <u>**EXAM APPROACH TO UCC REMEDIES ISSUES**</u> *****
- i. Determine which party is the non-breaching one, i.e., will it be buyer or seller that will bring the suit?
- ii. If it is buyer who is bringing the suit:
    1. At least check to see whether replacement of the good will be burdensome enough to qualify for specific performance
    2. If not (as is usually the case), then determine whether the buyer has or does not have goods tendered by the seller
        - a. If the buyer does not have the goods, recovery is based on:
            - i. Cover if the buyer reasonably purchases replacement goods, OR

      ii. Market differential damages if the buyer does not go into the marker and purchase replacement goods
     b. If the buyer retains the goods, the suit will be based for breach of warranty, and recovery will be based on the value of what the buyer was promised less the value of what he received
  iii. If it is the seller who is bringing suit:
    1. Check to see whether the seller can bring an action for price
    2. If not (as is usually the case), then recovery is based on:
     a. The price received upon the resale of the goods less the contract price
     b. The market differential, **but**
     c. If either of these methods do not put the seller in the position he would have been in had the contract been performed, as is likely the case with the **lost volume seller**, then lost profit recovery is allowed

About The Author

Kevin Lomax, JD graduated from a top three undergraduate school and then attended a top ten law school, where he graduated near the top of his class. Kevin is not the author's real name, as he wishes to stay anonymous at his current place of employment. Kevin suggests that you watch movies such as *The Firm* and *The Devil's Advocate* because these movies only hint at the "fun" that will await you in big law life upon graduating from law school.

www.ingramcontent.com/pod-product-compliance
Lightning Source LLC
Chambersburg PA
CBHW080939220526
45465CB00008BA/3096